Analysing the Evidence

Sources in British Social and Economic History

Robert Wolfson and J. F. Aylett

Hodder & Stoughton

LONDON SYDNEY AUCKLAND TORONTO

Acknowledgements

The publishers would like to acknowledge the following for permission to reproduce material in this volume:
Paul Cave Publications Ltd for 'Bunts for the oven – and a saw to cut the salt' by H W Harding from *Hampshire Magazine* (1973); Collins Educational for the extracts from *Making Modern Britain* by Christopher Culpin (1987) and *A Pageant of History* by R W Pirton (1962); David and Charles Publishers PLC for the extract from *The Early Factory Masters* by Stanley D Chapman (1967); *The Early Times* for the article about Margaret Thatcher and her Clean Up Litter Campaign, 1988; Holmes McDougall Limited for the extract from *Medicine Through Time* by Joe Scott (1987); MacMillan Limited for the extract about Florence Nightingale from *The MacMillan Encyclopedia* (1987); Reader's Digest/Doubleday Inc for the extract from 'The Soldiers' Angel' from *Great Lives, Great Deeds* by Mary R S Andrews (1965); *Sunday Sport* for 'Green-fingered aliens shocker', 13 November 1988; *The Sunday Telegraph* for 'Cruise Children fly to reunion', 23 October 1988.

The publishers would like to thank the following for their permission to reproduce copyright illustrations:
B T Batsford Limited, p 50 bottom; The Bodleian Library per 2705 d.407 vol 28, pp 14 bottom, 37 top; From the collections of Bolton Museums and Art Gallery, pp 13, 14 middle; The British Library, p 37 bottom; British Museum Fotomas Index, p 35; The Library of Congress, Washington, p 26 bottom; Durham Record Office D/PS/3/40 (Darlington Branch), p 28; Mary Evans Picture Library, p 34; The Folio Society, p 58 left; The Hulton-Deutsch Collection, pp 4, 5, 20, 21, 24 bottom, 26 top, 27 bottom, 48 top, 49 top, 50 top, 59, 66, 70, 72 left; Illustrated London News Picture Library, p 65 top; D Knights-Whittome, p 51 right; Lancashire County Museum Service, p 52 bottom; The Mansell Collection, pp 39, 47 both, 62, 64, 73 top, 74; Paul Mellon Centre, p 14 top; National Film Archive, London, pp 55, 56; Reproduced from the Blackett (Matfen) MSS in the Northumberland Record Office, p 27 top; Private Eye, p 43; Reproduced by permission of Punch, pp 15 left, 44 both, 45 left; Quarry Bank Mill Trust Archives, p 73 bottom; Reproduced by Gracious permission of Her Majesty The Queen, p 46; Rex Features, p 52 top; The Salisbury and South Wiltshire Museum, pp 29, 54 bottom; Courtesy of the Trustees of the Science Museum, London, p 6 all; M J Stone Collection, p 53; University of London Library, p 49 bottom; By Courtesy of The Trustees of The Victoria and Albert Museum, p 65 bottom; Warwickshire County Libraries, p 24 top; Wiltshire Library and Museum Service, p 11 bottom.

Every effort has been made to trace copyright holders of material reproduced in this book. Any rights not acknowledged here will be acknowledged in subsequent printings if notice is given to the publishers.

British Library Cataloguing in Publication Data

Wolfson, Robert
   Analysing the evidence for social and economic history.
   1. Historical sources
   I. Title II. Aylett, J.F. (John F.)
   907

ISBN 0 340 51008 0

First published 1990

© 1990 Robert Wolfson and J. F. Aylett

Original artwork by John Stuart Clark.
Typeset by Taurus Graphics, Abingdon
Printed in Great Britain for Hodder and Stoughton Educational, a division of Hodder and Stoughton Ltd, Mill Road, Dunton Green, Sevenoaks, Kent by Thomson Litho Ltd, East Kilbride

Contents

Myth and fact often get very intertwined
(Asa Briggs, 1985)

—1—
Sources for Social and Economic History

In your history lessons, you will already have discovered the great variety of sources that historians can use. The pictures on pages 2 and 3 will remind you of many of them. Study them now before answering the questions below.

EXERCISES

1 If you were asked to find out about the death of King Harold in 1066 and about the General Strike in 1926, which do you think would be easier? You must assume that the modern books written about each event do not exist, or that you are searching for fresh information. Write down two lists, one headed 'Sources of information for the death of King Harold' and the other 'Sources of information for the General Strike'. The drawings on the next two pages may give you ideas.

The death of King Harold, from the Bayeux Tapestry.

Special constables during the General Strike of 1926.

PERSONAL EVIDENCE	GOVERNMENT AND OFFICIAL RECORDS	NEWSPAPERS AND MAGAZINES

Diaries

Reports of parliamentary debates

Reports of what happened

Letters

Government investigations and reports

Editorial comments

Biographies

Politicians' speeches

Features and reviews

Oral history

Statistics

Letters to the editor

VISUAL EVIDENCE	ARTEFACTS	OTHER FORMS OF EVIDENCE

Paintings, drawings and cartoons

Fashions

Literary

Films and TV

Tools and machines

Songs and ballads

Photographs

Trains and cars

Radio broadcasts

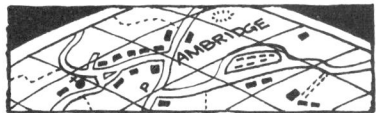

Maps and charts

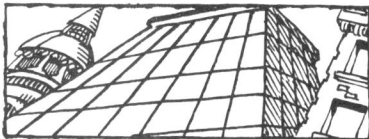

Buildings

Advertisements

Stamps

Personal possessions

Historical sites, farms and factories

2 In question 1, you will have found that there are many more sources for studying recent history. This can make it much easier to find out what happened, because more information is available. But now try answering this question: In what ways does having more sources make the historian's task more *difficult*?

What are we trying to find out?

Of course, historians want to know 'what happened'. This is called making a **narrative** of events. But they hope to do other things too. First, they have to decide, from all the things that have happened, which was important enough to go into the history books. The next question illustrates this problem.

EXERCISE

3 The following six events were all reported in the first issue of *The Sunday Times* in 1822. Which do you think was the most important news that Sunday? Give reasons for your choice.

(a) Boxing match in Epping Forest ended in the twentieth round.

(b) Slave-owner, aged 74, sentenced to death for raping a young slave.

(c) Mrs Garrick, widow of the great actor, died.

(d) Why *The Sunday Times* is being published.

(e) Father charges 10-year-old son with robbing him.

(f) Two houses deliberately burned in Ireland.

No doubt you found it very difficult to decide. It is too easy to pick what seems to us in the twentieth century to be the most

Boxing match.

interesting item. Then, we assume that it must have been equally interesting to people over 150 years ago.

In fact, the main item that Sunday was (d). *The Sunday Times* wanted to tell its readers why it was being published. That tells us why the news item was printed – and why it was at the top of the front page.

But another question needs to be asked: 'Important to *whom*?' The family of the little girl who was raped had other matters on their mind. So, too, did Bill Cropley, whose young son had been robbing him for months.

Newspapers, like historians, have to decide what to print. No newspaper prints all the news. The editor decides what to miss out. No historian prints all the details. History books would be too heavy to carry if they did. Historians, too, must make choices.

As well as having to choose which events to write about, historians ask other questions too:

• *Why* did things happen as they did?

• *What* effects did events have on people?

• *How* did they affect later events?

• *What were the events like* for the people who lived through them?

—2—
Primary and Secondary Sources

You probably already know the difference between primary and secondary sources. Primary sources come from the time of an event. Secondary sources are written or made after the event.

However, this does not make them exactly the same as 'first-hand' and 'second-hand' information. For example, an author of a diary might hear about an event from someone else; this would make his diary entry second-hand. Yet, if he wrote the entry at the time of the event, it is still a primary source.

George Stephenson.

In this chapter, some of the other difficulties of primary and secondary sources are examined. The first question checks your understanding of the basic distinction between primary and secondary sources.

EXERCISE

Sources on early railways, 1825–1830.

1 Make two lists, one headed 'Primary sources' and the other 'Secondary sources'. Then place each of these sources under the correct heading:
(a) A letter written by George Stephenson in 1823.
(b) A television programme about the Stockton to Darlington Railway.
(c) A local newspaper of 1825, announcing the opening of the Stockton to Darlington Railway.
(d) A painting of George Stephenson, made in his lifetime.
(e) A train ticket from 1830.
(f) *Rocket 150*, published in 1980, to celebrate the 150th anniversary of the opening of the Liverpool and Manchester Railway.
(g) A map, made in 1938, showing early railways in the north of England.
(h) The Act of Parliament (1826) which allowed the Liverpool and Manchester Railway to be built.
(i) A wreath laid in 1930, in memory of William Huskisson.
(j) A radio interview with a historian about I K Brunel.

various other minor changes. The reason was that the *Rocket* was a working engine. In 1837, it was bought by Messrs Thompson of Kirkhouse for £300. When they no longer needed it, they gave it to a museum in 1862.

Sadly, by then, it had lost quite a few of its parts. So what you can see in the photograph is, strictly speaking, the *remains* of the *Rocket*. Does this mean it is a secondary source, rather than a primary one?

However, it is not always that easy to decide whether a source is primary or secondary. Look at the two pictures above. The photograph on the left shows George Stephenson's *Rocket*, as it looks today. You can still see it in the Science Museum. It must be a primary source.

Or is it? Look at the print on the right. It, too, shows the *Rocket*, as it appeared at the Rainhill Trials in 1829. You should be able to spot three main differences.

So what is the engine in the photograph? It has a plate on its side which says *Rocket*, yet it is not the same as the one in the print.

Like many mysteries, this one has a simple solution. By 1832, the *Rocket* had undergone changes. A smoke box had been added and the cylinders had been lowered. The beam at the front was also added at some stage.

That is not the end of the story. If you look at the two pictures, you will see

Another Rocket*? This one is definitely a secondary source. It is a replica, built by Robert Stephenson & Co. It is the closest we can now get to what the original locomotive looked like.*

2 For each of the following, decide whether it is a primary or a secondary source. In each case, give reasons for your decision.

(a) A television programme about the first men on the moon in 1969, made in 1989. It included TV and radio news broadcasts from 1969 and interviews with the astronauts, and was introduced by a historian.

(b) An interview with Edward Heath in 1986, about his time as British Prime Minister in the 1970s.

(c) A book called *The Thirties, Turbulent Times*. It contains photographs and writing about the 1930s, all taken or written during that decade, and collected and published by an author in 1982.

So maybe it is not so easy to put sources into a simple category of 'primary' or 'secondary'. You may prefer to see them as two extremes of a continuum, or the ends of a line.

At one end are those that are purely primary (such as an eye-witness report); at the other are those that are purely secondary. Between the two extremes lie many sources which are a mixture of both.

You may be asked: Which are more useful – primary or secondary sources? Your first reaction may well be to say, 'Primary, because they come from the actual time.'

You might go on to argue that people who were there when something happened are bound to have a better idea of what went on . . . Or that photographs of an event must be accurate and cannot have been altered . . . Or that an actual law or government report must be accurate because it is sure to be a 'true' version.

However, a little more thought may lead you to change your mind. How many eye-witnesses will have seen the *whole* of an event? And how many will have stayed calm enough to give an accurate account afterwards?

Even a film or photographs will only show part of the event. Also, as Chapter 9 explains, there are many ways in which they may not tell the 'truth'. And, while an official report may seem to give a full and objective account, it may be that the government has made sure that only *its* version appears.

People putting together secondary sources have one great advantage. They can study many primary, and other secondary, sources. So their books can give an overview of the whole event from many different viewpoints. Also, writers can present the information in a way that is suitable for the particular readers. They can choose the right style, or present the different viewpoints of the people who were there.

Above all, it is important to consider what the sources are being used for. Are you trying to create a narrative? Or to find out why things happened as and when they did? Or are you hoping to discover the thoughts and feelings of some of the people who lived through an event? In many ways, this will influence your answer to the question of which type of source is most useful.

EXERCISE

3 You should work on this exercise in groups, using the ideas above and as many of your own ideas as you can. Draw out and complete a chart like that below. Then, present and explain your ideas to other groups.

	Advantages	Disadvantages
Primary sources		
Secondary sources		

—3—
Subjectivity and Objectivity

Having looked at the different types of evidence and considered the questions that historians try to answer, this chapter examines some important differences between sources.

Any historical source *may*

- only give facts about what happened

- only tell you how an individual or group of people felt about an event

- only give the author's opinion

- only make judgements about people or events

Many sources do more than one of these things. They give the reader a mixture of fact, opinion and judgement and the reader then has to sort out which is which. It is important to be able to do this. Otherwise, there is the danger of accepting one person's opinion as fact.

Different kinds of source help to answer different questions. For example, a diary or letter is not the best source for finding out exactly what happened. Nor does an Act of Parliament give you much idea of how people felt about a law, or what opinions people had of it.

EXERCISES

The Agricultural Revolution: Enclosures

Answer the following questions by studying Sources 3a–3e.

1 Write down which of these sources, if any, is stating:
(a) facts only
(b) opinions only
(c) feelings only
(d) judgements only.

2 For each of the sources that you have not included in your answer to question 1, copy out:
(a) those parts that record only facts
(b) those parts that are giving feelings or opinions
(c) those parts that are making judgements.

SOURCE 3a

(Arthur Young: *An Inquiry into the Propriety of Applying Wastes*, 1801)

Go to the alehouse of an old enclosed country, and there you will see the origin of poverty and poor rates. For whom are they to be sober? For whom are they to save? (Such are their questions.) . . .

If enclosures were beneficial to the poor, rates would not rise as in other parishes after an act to enclose. The poor in these parishes may say, and with truth, *Parliament may be tender of property; all I know is, I had a cow, and an act of Parliament has taken it from me.* And thousands may make this speech with truth.

SOURCE 3b

(Rev D Davies: *The Case of the Labourers in Husbandry*, 1795)

Thousands of families . . . have been gradually

reduced to the class of **day-labourers**. But day-labourers are sometimes in want of work, and are sometimes unable to work; and in either case their resort is the parish. It is a fact, that thousands of parishes have not now half the number of farmers which they had formerly. And in proportion as the number of farming families has decreased, the number of poor families has increased.

SOURCE 3c

(From a **tenant farmer**'s letter to Lord Hardwicke's steward, 1734)

Sir, [most] of the Nation being soe much Improved by Inclosures that I think there was never more Reason for wee at Hardwick to make some to Keep up the Rents of our Lands.

SOURCE 3d

(Sir F M Eden: *The State of the Poor*, 1797)

The advantages which cottagers and poor people derive from commons and wastes, are rather apparent than real; . . . they waste their time . . . in picking up a few dry sticks, or in grubbing up, on some bleak moor, a little furze, or heath.

Their starved pig or two, together with a few wandering **goslings** . . . are dearly paid for, by the care and time, and bought food, which are necessary to rear them.

Add to this, that as commons, and wastes . . . are undoubtedly the property, not of cottagers, but of the landowners; these latter, by the present wretched system, are thus made to maintain their poor, in a way the most costly to themselves, and the least beneficial to the poor.

SOURCE 3e

(John Byng, *The Torrington Diaries*, 1782)

Woman: Alackaday Sir, [enclosure] was a bad job, and ruined all us poor folk.
Lord Torrington: Why so?
Woman: Because we had our garden, our bees, our share of a flock of sheep, and the feeding of our geese. And could cut turf for our fuel. Now that is gone! My cottage with many others is

pulled down and the poor are sadly put to it to get a house to put their heads in.

The words *objectivity* and *subjectivity*, used as the title of this chapter, can now be explained. If something is *objective*, it records only the *facts* of what happened, and gives little or no idea of feelings or opinions.

The reports of the daily proceedings of Parliament (known as Hansard) and encyclopaedias, are the kinds of sources that are regarded as objective. Hansard simply records exactly what was said – even the cheers and boos – by all members of Parliament. Of course, this does not mean that the speeches of the MPs were objective.

Encyclopaedias are less simple. The editor has to decide what information to include, and what to leave out. In deciding this, the editor has to decide what is and is not important (see also page 38). In doing this, he or she will present a particular view of a person or event, by including or excluding certain information. This is sometimes called 'subjectivity by selection'.

If something is subjective, it might give an opinion or view without including any facts at all. For instance, in Source 3e above, 'Alackaday, Sir, [enclosure] was a bad job and ruined all us poor folk', is simply an opinion.

Alternatively, a subjective source can use facts in a particular way. 'Thousands of families . . . have been gradually reduced to the class of day-labourers . . .' (Source 3b) contains fact, but also suggests the author's opinion – he is opposed to enclosure because it has made more people poor. It is, therefore, a subjective statement even though it is factual.

Subjectivity and objectivity can now be linked to the ideas about primary and secondary sources examined in Chapter 2. Historical sources can be placed on two 'scales', one showing the extent to which they are primary or secondary, the other the extent to which they are objective or subjective.

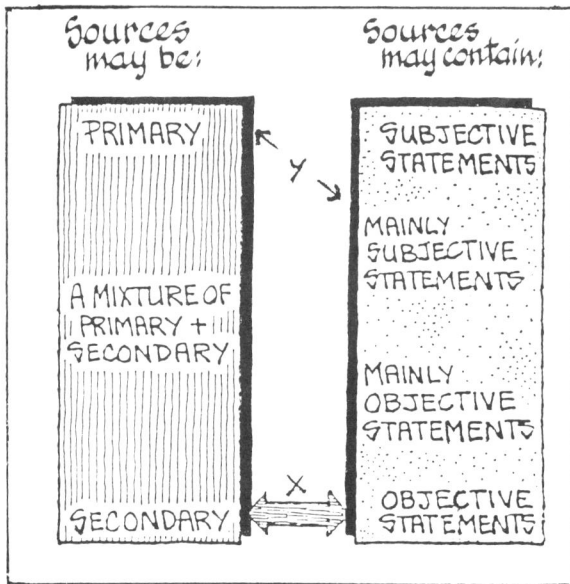

The diagram above will help to make this clearer. For instance, suppose we wrote 'Jethro Tull invented a seed drill'. This would be an objective statement, as it contains no ideas of how we feel about it. It is also a secondary source, as it was written a long time after the event. This is shown by the x on the diagram.

On the other hand, if we found a contemporary letter in which a farmer wrote 'Tull's seed drill made a huge difference to my farm', that would be placed at y on the diagram. It is a primary source, and mainly presents an opinion of the invention.

EXERCISE

3 Draw the diagram above. Take each of the Sources 3a to 3e and indicate where you think each should fit on the diagram.

Historians also ask other questions of their sources:
● Are there gaps in the evidence?

Few sources will tell us absolutely everything we need to know. The problem is to judge how important the gaps are. They might be so great as to make the source useless. It might be that the facts included or excluded present only one point of view. It may even be that some things have been deliberately left out because they do not support the author's point of view.

An ACT *for Confirming the Inclosure, Division, and Exchanges of several Lands and Grounds lying in the Common Fields of* Wollesthorpe, *near* Belvoir Castle, *in the County of* Lincoln.

An Enclosure Act.

● Do the sources present a national or a local picture?

Some sources present an accurate and detailed picture of events, but it may be limited to one area of the country. Many authors only wrote about enclosure, for example, in the area they knew. The historian then has to ask if this picture is typical of the whole country, or just how one area was affected.

Equally, some authors will write about a national trend or event as though it happened in the same way everywhere. In fact, it was often the case that different places were affected quite differently (see Sources 3f–3h opposite).
● Are the sources **consistent**?

Some sources **contradict** themselves in different places; when they do this, they are called *inconsistent*. Often, one source will be contradicted by another on the same subject, especially when opinions and judgements are given. This is shown by the next three sources on enclosure:

SOURCE 3f

(Robert Unwin: *Britain since 1700*, 1986)

The cottagers and squatters, those villagers who had the least right to land, suffered most from the enclosure of fields and the break-up of waste and common land. Enclosure resulted in the use of more efficient farming methods and machinery, which brought unemployment and hardship to many farm labourers.

SOURCE 3g

(Gloucester Record Office: *Inclosure in Gloucestershire*, 1976)

The population [of Aston Blank] continued to rise from about 200 people in 40 households at the time of inclosure, to 295 in 60 households a generation later in 1831. This reflects the general population rise in the country [and] the conversion of **pasture** to **arable** which required more farm labourers.

A rich farmer with his family.

Ambrose Matthews and his wife, photographed in 1900. He was a farm labourer, earning between 50p and 70p a week.

SOURCE 3h

(T Brown: *General View of the Agriculture of the County of Derby*, 1794)

I know there are places where common arable fields have been inclosed, laid down in pasture, and neglected; less ploughing done, and perhaps fewer labourers employed, after the inclosure; but this very rarely happens ... Wherever inclosures are turned to the most advantage, I will [argue] they require an increase of capital, attention and labour; and [so] the number of labouring hands are not [reduced].

EXERCISES

4 For each of Sources 3f to 3h, write down whether it is primary or secondary.
5 (a) How did enclosure affect Aston Blank?
   (b) How does Source 3g prove Source 3f is wrong? (Think carefully.)
6 (a) How does Source 3h support Source 3f?
   (b) How does Source 3h support Source 3g?
   (c) Does that mean that both Sources 3f and 3g are correct? Explain your answer.

Finding differences like this leads the historian to investigate further – to check other sources and to look into the background of the authors.

If they find contradictions, historians will question the *reliability* of the source and its author. It may still be *useful*, though, because it will tell the historian something about the subject that can be checked and balanced by different evidence.

Inventions in the Cotton Industry

Read the following sources about the cotton industry and try to compare the information as you read. Then answer the questions which follow:

SOURCE 3i

(R Cochlin: *Life and Work from 1700 to the Present*, 1978)

The real changes in spinning came in the 1760s, when a weaver from Blackburn, named James Hargreaves, invented a machine that was able to spin six threads at once. It was called the Spinning Jenny, named after his wife . . . . Hargreaves had meant it to be a small machine, to be used in the cottages, but the idea was developed until it could spin eighty threads at once.

SOURCE 3j

(R L Hills: *Cotton Spinning*, 1977)

One day in about 1763, a spinning wheel in James Hargreaves' home was knocked over accidentally. As it lay on its side, still rotating, it inspired him to try making a spinning machine.

SOURCE 3k

(L F Hobley: *Living and Working*, 1964)

The first commercially successful invention in spinning was that of the spinning jenny by James Hargreaves, a Blackburn weaver. When first patented in 1767 it spun eight threads instead of one. Later it was improved to spin over a hundred.

SOURCE 3l

(Christopher Culpin: *Making Modern Britain*, 1987)

James Hargreaves was a weaver and carpenter from Blackburn, Lancashire. A 'jenny' is just an engine or any sort of machine. He is said to have got the idea in 1764 from seeing a spinning wheel . . . knocked over and carry on spinning. Hargreaves' first jenny had eight spindles. The version he patented in 1770 had sixteen.

EXERCISES

7 (a) In what ways do the sources differ on the date of Hargreaves's invention?
(b) Do they agree on how it got its name? Explain your answer.
(c) How do they differ over the number of threads it could spin?
8 What questions would you ask of the authors to try to find out why they differ on these points?

Historians will also ask themselves if the sources are biased.

If you look up the word 'bias' in a dictionary, you will find it means 'inclination, **prejudice** or influence'. Usually, historians use it to mean 'one-sided' or 'written from only one point of view'.

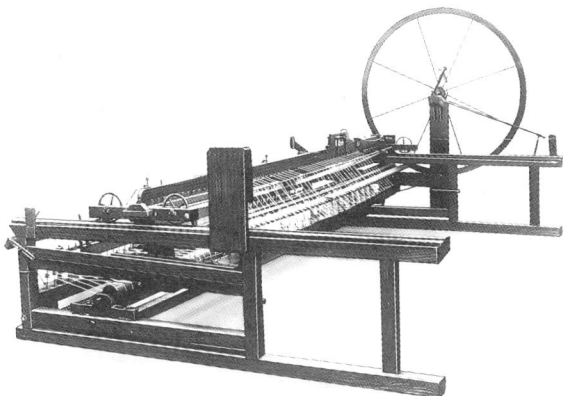

A Spinning Jenny.

It is often thought that some authors are bound to be biased because of who they are, or were. For example, many people assume that a Conservative MP will *always* say nice things about other Conservatives – and unpleasant things about Labour MPs! Although this can be true, many people are able to give credit to the talents of their opponents and can see both sides of a debate.

Others will argue that we are all biased in some way. Everyone has their own set of beliefs and opinions. These will sometimes show through in their writing, whether they like it or not.

Even so, biased sources can be of great value to historians. They should not simply be dismissed. The opinions of writers can help historians to understand how people felt about events or to see why they happened as they did.

They often contain factual information and ideas which should be balanced by comparing them with other sources. Then the historian can begin to build up an overall picture.

9 Study the set of sources below and on the next page about Sir Richard Arkwright and then answer these questions:

(a) What impression of Arkwright do you get from reading *only* Sources 3m, 3n and 3o?

(b) In what way(s) does Source 3p present a different view of Arkwright?

(c) What impression of Arkwright do you get from the painting?

(d) Which, if any, of these sources (including the pictures) do you regard as biased? Explain your answer.

(e) Why do you think the songs (3n and 3o) were written?

(f) Do these sources have any use? Explain your answer.

SOURCE 3m

(Joseph Farington: *Diary*, not published until 1922)

August 23 – We went to Church at Cromford where is a Chapel built abt. 3 years and ½ ago by Mr Arkwright. On each side the Organ a gallery in which about 50 Boys were seated. These children are employed in Mr Arkwright's work in the week-days, and on Sundays attend a school where they receive education. They came to Chapel in regular order and looked healthy & well & were decently cloathed & clean. They were attended by an Old Man their School Master – To this school girls also go for the same purpose, and alternately with the Boys go to Church the Boys on one Sunday – the girls on the next following. – Whichever are not at Chapel are at the School, to which they both go every Sunday both morning and afternoon. The whole plan appears to be such as to do Mr Arkwright great credit.

SOURCE 3n

(The song over the page was sung by the villagers at Cromford each year at prize-giving time. From *The Torrington Diaries*)

Come let us all here join in one,
And thank him for all favours done;
Let's thank him for all favours still
Which he hath done beside the mill.

Modestly drink liquor about,
And see whose health you can find out;
This will I chuse before the rest
Sir Richard Arkwright is the best.

SOURCE 3o

(Verses 1 and 5 of a song sung at Cromford in
October 1778, on the occasion of a feast given
by Arkwright)

Ye num'rous Assembly that make up this Throng
Spare your Mirth for a Moment and list to my
song,
The bounties let's sing, that our Master belong,
    At the Cotton-Mills now at Cromford,
    The famous renown'd Cotton-Mills.

To our noble Master, a Bumper then fill,
The matchless Inventor of this Cotton-Mill,
Each toss off his Glass with a hearty Good-will,
    With huzza for the Mills now at Cromford,
    All join with a jovial Huzza.

SOURCE 3p

(Stanley D Chapman: *The Early Factory Masters*,
1967. He is discussing life at Cromford)

The inns and the market-place, and perhaps the
church, chapel and Sunday-schools too, provided
a full measure of social opportunities. This is the
side that has been most noticed, but there is
another.

Even in 1816, not more than one in five of the
factory-hands got a tea-break in their thirteen-
hour day. And for something like twenty-two
years [until] the death of Arkwright, a large
number of boys – at one time there were 164 of
them – were employed on night shifts, and
though they were paid 'extravagant wages' they
'were extremely **dissipated**'.

More evidence is necessary before any
conclusions can be drawn. The best that can be
said for Arkwright in this context is that many
other cotton mills . . . worked their machinery
twenty-four hours a day up to about 1796.

A painting of Sir Richard Arkwright.

Richard Arkwright once ran a barber's shop here.

*This is the earliest known picture of Arkwright's first mill
at Cromford.*

Racial bias

Most books on social history in the eighteenth and nineteenth centuries make little mention of immigrants, except for the Irish. If you look at the pictures in a social and economic textbook, you will find that they are practically all of white people. Only in the second half of the twentieth century do pictures of other people begin to appear.

Yet this is not a true picture of Britain at that time. By the mid-eighteenth century, some 20 000 black people were living in the country. Many were servants; most were poor. However, some were better-off; Ignatius Sancho, for instance, was a popular author.

Numbers went down in the nineteenth century after the slave trade was banned. Some emigrated but most stayed in Britain. One Jamaican nurse became a heroine in her own day and eventually settled in Britain. She was Mary Seacole, famous for helping troops during the Crimean War.

London was already attracting people from all over the British Empire. More than half the **tract** sellers on the London streets in the middle of the nineteenth century were blacks or Asians.

A Hindu tract-seller in London, mid-nineteenth century.

During the second world war, many people volunteered to come to Britain and help in the war effort. Over 15 000 came from the West Indies; some worked in factories, others with RAF ground crews. A few became air raid wardens.

This is where the problem of 'subjectivity by selection' comes in. If a book can only print one picture of air raid wardens, should it show black wardens or only white ones?

To show only black wardens might suggest that there were more of them than was really the case. But to show only white wardens might make people think (as many people do) that there were no black ones. Which would be the right choice for a historian to make?

OUR OWN VIVANDIERE.

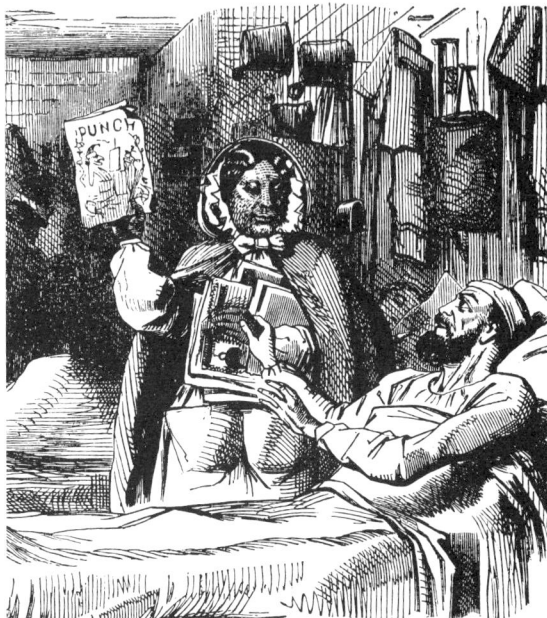

Mary Seacole in a Punch *cartoon of 1857.*

Black air-raid wardens in St Pancras, 1942.

EXERCISES

10 Why do you think most books include little or nothing about black people in nineteenth century Britain?

11 Find out what you can about either Ignatius Sancho or Mary Seacole from other books, including encyclopaedias. In your research, record which books tell you something about them, and which tell you nothing.

—4—
Government and Official Records

There is a vast store of government records, covering the history of the last three hundred years. When textbooks quote from these they only use a fraction of what exists.

There are many different kinds and types of government and official records. In the section that follows, some of these different types will be referred to in examining the case of the workhouse at Andover.

In March 1846, Parliament decided to set up a Committee to inquire into the running of the workhouse at Andover. A Select Committee is a group of people chosen to study a particular problem.

The members of the Committee usually interview people and visit the place they are concerned about. They then publish a report, which usually ends with a set of recommendations. These advise Parliament, and others, what to do about the problem.

The report was published in August 1846. It was 1000 pages long and contained 20 000 questions and answers. In addition, there were 30 appendices to back up the report itself.

You could still read the full report today in the British Museum. Few people, of course, ever have. Most people at the time made do with a summary of it in their newspaper.

SOURCE 4a

(From appendix 26 to the *Report of the Select Committee on Andover Union*, 1946) This picture showed a crusher and box used by the men in the workhouse. It was their job to crush animal bones.

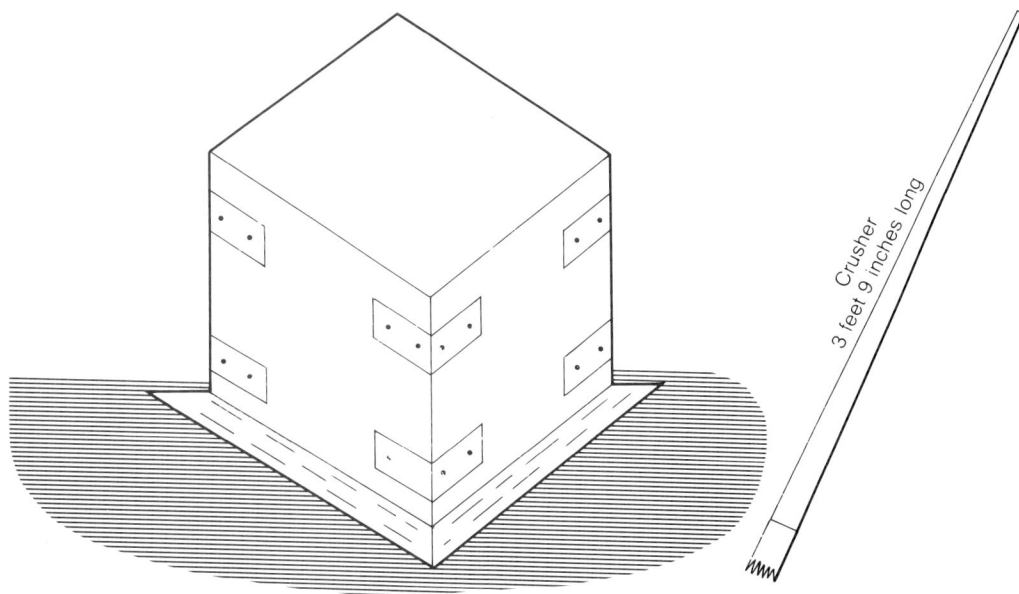

3 feet 9 inches long Crusher

Andover Workhouse, as it looks today.

The Select Committee's report was not the only official document about the workhouse. Those responsible for the workhouse had to issue annual reports. This was the report that the local Guardians had to produce each year. The first of these included a long list of the workhouse master's duties.

SOURCE 4b

(These are just a few of the master's duties. From the first *Annual Report of the Board of Guardians*)

The following shall be the duties of the master of the workhouse:

1. To admit **paupers** into the workhouse, and to cause them to be examined by the medical officer, and to cleanse, clothe, and place them in the proper wards, according to the regulations herein established.

3. To read prayers to the paupers before breakfast and after supper every day, or cause them to be read, at which all the inmates must attend; [except those who are opposed on religious grounds].

4. To inspect and call over the names of all the paupers immediately after morning prayers every day, and see that each individual is clean, and in a proper state.

6. To visit the sleeping wards of the first, second, and third classes at 11 o'clock every day, to see that they have been all duly cleaned and properly ventilated.

7. To see that the meals of the paupers are properly dressed and served, and to superintend the distribution thereof.

8. To say or cause to be said grace before and after meals.

9. To see that the dining halls, tables, and seats, are cleaned after each meal.

10. To visit all the wards of the male paupers at nine o'clock every night, and see that all the male paupers are in bed, and that all fires and lights are extinguished.

11. To receive from the gatekeeper the keys of the workhouse at nine o'clock every night, and to deliver them to him again at six o'clock every morning.

This was followed by a list of the matron's duties. In addition, the Andover Workhouse had a list of Orders and Regulations. These were also published in the Andover Union's first Annual Report.

What is remarkable about these rules is how detailed they were. No aspect of workhouse life went unnoticed.

SOURCE 4c

(Workhouse hours. Printed in the first Annual Report)

	Hour of rising	Interval for Breakfast	Time for setting to work	Interval for Dinner	Time for leaving off work	Interval for supper	Time for going to bed
From 25th March to 29th September	6 o'clock	6.30 to 7	7 o'clock	12 to 1	6 o'clock	6 to 7	8
From 29th September to 25th March	7 o'clock	7.30 to 8	8 o'clock	12 to 1	6 o'clock	6 to 7	8

Parliament had set up the Committee because rumours had been spreading in Andover in 1845. The rumours said that men employed on breaking bones in the bone-yard were so hungry that they were eating them. These rumours seemed to be true. So one of the Guardians, Hugh Mundy, wrote to his MP.

That summer, another MP asked a question about Andover Workhouse in the House of Commons.

Today, all debates in the House of Commons are recorded word for word. These complete accounts have been published since 1909 and are called *Hansard*. This was the name of the printer who had been publishing details since 1811.

So records of what was said in Parliament about the Andover Workhouse do exist. However, they are not exact accounts of the debates. Today, there is simply no way of knowing for sure how accurate they are.

However, one source will give a flavour of the language used. This source *is* accurate because it was a motion which was agreed by MPs.

SOURCE 4d

(House of Commons motion, March 5 1846)

Ordered, That a Select Committee be appointed to inquire into the Administration of the Poor Laws in the Andover Union, and also into the Management of the Union Workhouse; and into the Conduct of the Poor-Law Commissioners, and their late Assistant Commissioner, Mr Parker, in reference to the Two Investigations held at Andover; and into all the Circumstances under which the Poor-Law Commissioners called upon Mr Parker to resign his Assistant Commissionership.

(The Poor Law **Commission** had already made its own inquiries into the workhouse. It is these to which the motion refers).

Hansard

In 1700, the House of Commons kept its own record of debates. However, anyone publishing what was said in the House of Commons could be punished. So, in a way, debates were secret.

However, newspapers knew that readers wanted to know what politicians were saying. Reports were published, with politicians' names thinly disguised. For example, instead of printing the name 'Sir Robert Walpole', the paper printed 'Sir R-b-t W-lp-l-' instead.

Editors were taken to court and fined but the reports continued. However, reporters could not take notes in the House of Commons. They had to rely on their memories. As a result, these reports are not wholly reliable. A good speech probably meant it had been written by a good reporter!

Early in the nineteenth century, William Cobbett began printing details of debates. Newspapers began relying on teams of reporters. Each stayed just a short time in the House of Commons and wrote up his report at once. By combining these reports, Cobbett could produce a fairly accurate account.

In 1811, Cobbett sold the right to print these reports to his printer, T C Hansard. In 1854, a press gallery was provided in the House of Commons and note-taking became accepted. However, the reports of speeches were still summaries, until 1911.

The amount of details in the report made by the Select Committee gives us a good idea of how witnesses were questioned. Often, they were asked leading questions. This means that the questions gave information for the witness to include in his or her answer. You can read an extract on the next page.

The male ward in a typical workhouse of the 1840s.

SOURCE 4e

(Report of the Select Committee on Andover Union 1846. Anthony Antony, a workhouse porter, is being questioned by the Committee)

Q: Were the beggars always set to work?
A: Yes, in the morning.
Q: How long in the morning?
A: Till the men came out to breakfast.
Q: And although they were made to work they had no allowance of food before they went out?
A: No.
Q: In what state were the bones when they were admitted?
A: Some dry and some green.
Q: Have you seen the men gnaw the meat and gristle from the bones?
A: Yes.
Q: Witnessed it yourself?
A: Frequently; there was hardly a day but some of them were cutting the meat and gristle off the bones, and breaking them to get at the marrow.
Q: Most of the bones were in a stinking state?
A: Yes.

Q: Did you know that Mr Westlake, the surgeon, objected to the men crushing green bones?
A: Yes, he told McDougal (the workhouse master) that there should be no green bones brought.
Q: Did you hear Mr Westlake say so?
A: Yes.

The Poor Law Commission had been set up as a result of an Act of Parliament. All our laws are contained in Acts of Parliament. These laws provide yet more official documents for the social historian.

However, not all government reports are published. When the Cabinet meets to discuss affairs, **minutes** are kept of these meetings.

The Official Secrets Act allows the government to keep Cabinet minutes secret for thirty years. This means that Cabinet discussions in 1990 will not be published until the year 2020. Even then, some documents are not published if the Government feels it would be damaging to make them public.

(Report of the Select Committee on Andover
Union, 1846)

SELECT COMMITTEE ON ANDOVER UNION

No. 3 – Dietary for Able-bodied Persons above 9 Years of Age

		BREAKFAST		DINNER					SUPPER	
		Bread	Gruel	Cooked Meat	Vegetables	Soup	Bread	Cheese	Bread	Cheese
		oz	pints	oz	lb	pints	oz	oz	oz	oz
Sunday	Men	6	$1\frac{1}{3}$	–	–	–	7	2	6	$1\frac{1}{3}$
	Women	5	$1\frac{1}{2}$	–	–	–	6	$1\frac{1}{2}$	5	$1\frac{1}{2}$
Monday	Men	6	$1\frac{1}{3}$	–	–	–	7	2	6	$1\frac{1}{3}$
	Women	5	$1\frac{1}{2}$	–	–	–	6	$1\frac{1}{2}$	5	$1\frac{1}{2}$
Tuesday	Men	6	$1\frac{1}{3}$	8	$\frac{1}{3}$	–	–	–	6	$1\frac{1}{3}$
	Women	5	$1\frac{1}{2}$	6	$\frac{1}{2}$	–	–	–	5	$1\frac{1}{2}$
Wednesday	Men	6	$1\frac{1}{3}$	–	–	–	7	2	6	$1\frac{1}{3}$
	Women	5	$1\frac{1}{2}$	–	–	–	6	$1\frac{1}{2}$	5	$1\frac{1}{2}$
Thursday	Men	6	$1\frac{1}{3}$	–	–	$1\frac{1}{3}$	–	–	6	$1\frac{1}{3}$
	Women	5	$1\frac{1}{2}$	–	–	$1\frac{1}{2}$	–	–	5	$1\frac{1}{2}$
Friday	Men	6	$1\frac{1}{3}$	–	–	–	7	2	6	$1\frac{1}{3}$
	Women	5	$1\frac{1}{2}$	–	–	–	6	$1\frac{1}{2}$	5	$1\frac{1}{2}$
Saturday	Men	6	$1\frac{1}{3}$	Bacon: 5	$\frac{1}{3}$	–	–	–	6	$1\frac{1}{3}$
	Women	5	$1\frac{1}{2}$	4	$\frac{1}{2}$	–	–	–	5	$1\frac{1}{2}$

Old people of 60 years of age and upwards may be allowed 1 oz of tea, 7 oz of butter, and 8 oz of sugar per week, in lieu of gruel for breakfast, if deemed expedient to make this change.

Children under 9 years of age to be dieted at discretion; above 9 to be allowed the same quantities as women.

Sick to be dieted as directed by the medical officer.

The House of Commons in session.

The different types of government and official records that tell us about the Andover Workhouse scandal are shown in this diagram:

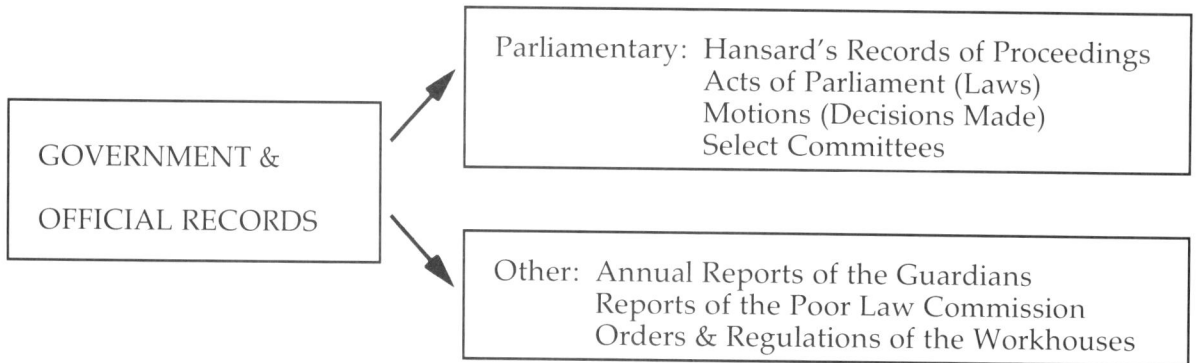

```
┌─────────────────────┐        ┌──────────────────────────────────────────┐
│                     │   ↗    │ Parliamentary: Hansard's Records of        │
│ GOVERNMENT &        │        │                Proceedings                 │
│                     │        │                Acts of Parliament (Laws)   │
│ OFFICIAL RECORDS    │        │                Motions (Decisions Made)    │
│                     │        │                Select Committees           │
│                     │   ↘    └──────────────────────────────────────────┘
└─────────────────────┘        ┌──────────────────────────────────────────┐
                               │ Other: Annual Reports of the Guardians     │
                               │        Reports of the Poor Law Commission  │
                               │        Orders & Regulations of the         │
                               │        Workhouses                          │
                               └──────────────────────────────────────────┘
```

EXERCISES

1 What do you think are (a) the advantages and (b) the disadvantages of government and official records for the historian? (Some of the things you might consider are length, detail, language, accuracy and amount.)
2 Do you think it is right that some aspects of government are kept secret? Explain your answer.
3 Using the evidence from Sources 4a to 4f, explain:
(a) Why a Select Committee was set up in 1846
(b) What the Committee discovered
(c) Which sources were especially helpful in telling you these things, and which less so.

4 (a) Read Source 4e carefully. At times, the questioner gives the porter information in his question. Write down two questions where he does this.
(b) Why must the historian treat the porter's answers with care? Explain your answer.
5 (a) What other *kinds* of evidence might be available on this topic?
(b) Which kind would tell you most about the feelings of the people in the workhouse?
(c) You are a reporter covering the Select Committee's interviews. What questions would you ask Anthony Antony?

—5—
Personal Documents

Diaries, letters, biographies and autobiographies are all forms of personal documents. They are valuable sources in helping historians to understand people. They can give historians an insight into a person's ideas and beliefs, and help them to understand why people acted as they did.

lived. They include details about everyday aspects of life, like travel and homes, clothes and food. From them, the social historian can build up a picture of life at a particular time in a particular place.

This is, however, one of the drawbacks of this type of evidence. Most people are concerned with their own lives and record details of things about them. They do not generally give us much idea about national events or characters. Source 5a is an example of this.

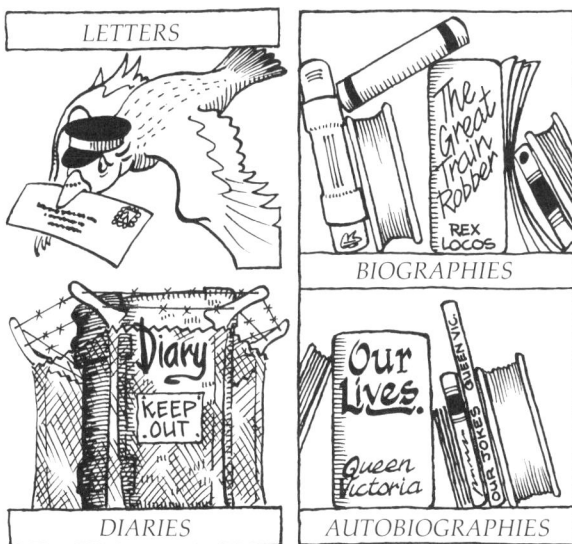

LETTERS

BIOGRAPHIES

DIARIES

AUTOBIOGRAPHIES

Diaries and letters

Personal documents are especially valuable for the study of social history. Diaries and letters help us to understand how people

SOURCE 5a

(*The Diary of William Andrews* (1850–66). William Andrews was a teenage **apprentice** when he began this diary. He went on to become a wealthy citizen of Coventry.)

Sunday Sep 1 1850:   Saw 3 women and 6 men baptised in the canal at Longford today.
Sep. 2:   Nuneaton railway opens today, saw the first train. Later in the day about 30 passengers had to ride on top of carriages, there not being room enough inside.
Sep. 3:   They began to fill Swanswell pool today.
Sep. 13:   Had a book 'The Nile Boat' presented to me at the annual meeting of School of Art by Thos. Cope Esq. as 2nd prize for ribbon design.
Sep. 15:   Visit the new Harbury cutting with C. Peters and Sidney Peters.
Oct. 14:   Swanswell is nearly completed.
Oct. 10:   Saw a large red beech tree removed from bottom of Hertford St. to cemetery today; the crowd cheered.

The opening of Nuneaton Railway, 1850.

Apr. 18: 5th Dragoons pass through Coventry en route for Turkey.

Apr. 26: A general fast on account of the war.

Oct. 2: Bells ring in Coventry today to celebrate the Alma victory and procession of a band and flags round the city.

Jan. 18 1855: About 80 wounded men from the Crimea arrive in Coventry from Liverpool where they had just landed.

Jan. 19: The wounded go by rail to Cheltenham and another lot arrive.

Mar. 21: General fast on account of the war.

As you can see, William Andrews jots down those things in his diary which interested him. None of these events was of national importance. Also, to understand local events, the reader needs other information. The people being baptised in the canal were Baptists. The railway was the Coventry, Bedworth and Nuneaton Railway, which had been started in 1847.

However, this does not mean the diary is of no use. William Andrews kept careful records of his annual earnings. From his diary, we can learn how his earnings rose:

1853 – £4 14 shillings 5 pence
1854 – £8.14.2
1855 – £21.7.9
1856 – £102.9.7
1857 – £111.8.6
1858 – £123.1.0

He recorded other details, too. By the end of 1859, he had saved £267. He would need this money when he later set up his own business.

Some details give us a glimpse of what was happening outside Coventry. In 1854, the Crimean War began. These entries are taken from his diaries:

Apr. 10–13 1854: Light Dragoons leave Coventry this morning for Turkey via Canterbury, Calais and Marseilles. Headquarters arrive from Birmingham.

Apr. 11: Headquarters leave, the band has broken up and put in ranks.

The Crimean War. This early photograph shows the cookhouse of the 8th Hussars.

The diary also provides glimpses of how people lived at the time:

Apr. 11 1856: Perceive a soreness in my throat tonight.

Apr. 12: Throat worse.

Apr. 13: Take a dose of rhubarb and repeat it in the evening.

Apr. 14: Throat worse.

Historians have to ask questions about the diaries and letters they use. Some letters and diaries are written with the intention of being published later.

As a result, their authors are more likely to have kept a careful record of times, places and people than the people who scribbled down their appointments or jotted their thoughts down each evening.

So, the diary kept for future publication is likely to be accurate. On the other hand, it may not be very objective. Its author could have been keen to give a favourable view of his or her part in events.

Letters, too, can be written in different circumstances and for a variety of purposes. Some are wholly personal, and are sent to friends or relations to keep in touch.

Others might be written to an MP or to a county councillor to try to win support for a particular cause. Then again, some letters are written to newspaper editors, in the hope that they will be published. The letter's style and content will be affected by (i) the circumstances in which the letter was written and (ii) the audience that the writer had in mind.

Equally, it is important to consider how much the author actually knew about the events he or she was writing about. Did they play a leading part in them? Or were they just a spectator? Was the person affected – for good or ill – by those events? And how did these effects influence the way the writer wrote of the events?

Only by seeking answers to these questions will the historian be able to establish the true value of the sources under study.

Road travel in the eighteenth century

As we have seen, diaries provide us with much information about daily life. This is particularly true of travel. The following extracts show what coach travel was like before the arrival of railways.

Educated people kept long and detailed diaries in the eighteenth and nineteenth centuries. The following extracts have all been shortened. The same is true of the letters in the section which follows.

SOURCE 5b

(John Byng: *The Torrington Diaries*, published in 1934–8)

(1790) At 7 o'clock in the morning I was pushed into the Manchester coach with three women:
one fat creature like a cook; One large, and younger, in a linen greatcoat; the third, older, in a blue greatcoat; and then learnt that we were to take up two more females at Islington: though the coach could but just hold four. When we had received and stowed our complement, much . . . discourse arose about London, its delights, and fine places . . . I skulked at a corner, and endured. The blue greatcoat, going to Manchester, was escorted by a young man, who rode on the coach box and drove; the large greatcoat, the cook, and the two young Islingtons were going to Derby; these last two had never been far from home. Change horses at Kitts-Inn; at Redburn; and at Dunstable; where dinner was prepared for us at 12 o'clock.

. . . The two large ladies, with an outside woman, [feasted] on a coarse, boiled leg of mutton, and a large neck of veal roasted; which I did also, and ordered, at *mine own charge*, a pint of red *wine* to entertain the ladies . . .

Night soon overshading us, the fat cook took from her pocket a pint bottle of [brandy], which I, and the old-blue, likewise, held to our mouths; whilst the refined party, complaining of head-aches, would only be cheered by salts. It was 11 o'clock when we reached Harborough; there changed horses; and at half past one we entered Leicester: my legs cramped double, and my hips sore.

SOURCE 5c

(Louis Simond: *Journal of a Tour and Residence in Great Britain, 1810–11*)

This morning I set out by myself for *town*, as London is called *par excellence*, in the stage coach, crammed inside and outside with passengers of all sexes, ages and conditions. We stopped more than 20 times on the road – the debates about the fare of the way-passengers – the settling themselves – the getting up, and the getting down, and damsels showing their legs in the operation, and tearing and muddying their petticoats – complaining and swearing – took an immense time. I never saw anything so ill managed.

A flying coach at the Bell Savage Inn, *where Parson Woodforde stayed.*

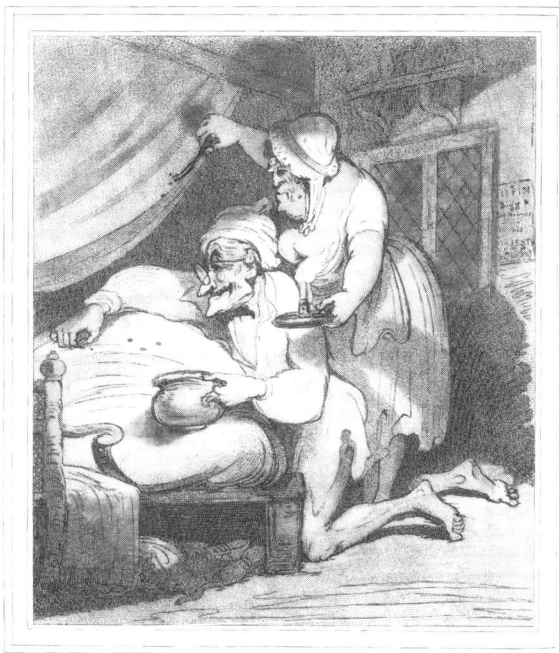

SUMMER AMUSEMENT.
BUGG HUNTING.

SOURCE 5d

(James Woodforde: *The Diary of a Country Parson*, published in 1926. He is making the journey from Norfolk to Somerset. At the moment described, he is in London, waiting for the Salisbury coach)

(1782) 31 May – We breakfasted, dined and spent the afternoon at our inn. For 2 inside places in the Salisbury coach pd. £2.2.0. For 1 outside place pd. £0.10.6. Paid and gave at the 'Bell Savage' for all of us abt. £1.15.0. They were very civil people at the Bell Savage Inn, and a very good house it is. About 10 o'clock at night we set off in the Salisbury coach from the same inn for Salisbury, and the coach guarded. I was bit terribly by the bugs last night, but did not wake me.
1 June – . . . I was terribly swelled in the face and hands by the bugs.

SOURCE 5e

(Joseph Ballard: *England in 1815, as seen by a Young Boston Merchant*, published in 1913)

We travelled all night. At dusk I was not a little surprised at [seeing] my fair fellow traveller, who was quite a pretty girl, take off her bonnet, tie on her night cap, and leisurely compose herself to sleep in one corner of the coach, where she made quite an interesting appearance.

After going with almost incredible swiftness, we arrived at Leeds at 6 o'clock in the morning, being at the rate of 8 miles and ⅓ each hour, including stoppages – a [speed] with which I never desire to travel again.

SOURCE 5f

(Sir Edward Blackett: accounts for travel expenses, August 2 and 3, 1827)

Date. 1827	PLACES. From London	Distance.	Horses.	Charge.			Hostlers.			Gates.			Postboys.			INNS.
		Miles.	No.	£.	s.	d.	£.	s.	d.	£.	s.	d.	£.	s.	d.	
Aug: 2nd	to Barnet	12	2	–	18	–					3	8		4		Green Man
	Hatfield	9	–		13	6					1	6		2	6	Salisbury arms
	Stevenage	12	–		18						1	6		4		Swan
Aug: 3rd	Biggleswade	14	–	1	1						1	6		4	6	Sun
	Eaton (Soton)	10			15							9		3		Cock
	Alconbury Hill	13			19	6					1			4		Wheatsheaf
	Wansford	16		1	4			6			2			4	6	Haycock
	Greetham	17			19	6					2			2	6	Royal Oak
	Grantham	18		1	1						3	6		5	6	George
	Newark	14		1	1						1	8		5		Lawton
	Scarthing -moor	11			16	6					1			4		Peale
				£10.7			6	0.19		£2.3	6						

EXERCISES

1 What do sources 5b–5f tell you about the following aspects of road travel?
 (a) the discomforts
 (b) the costs
 (c) the speed and distances travelled
 (d) the design of coaches.
2 Take each source in turn, and write down any weaknesses it has. Ask yourself these questions: Do they leave gaps? Are the sources consistent? Are they biased?
3 What other aspects of life, apart from coach travel, do these sources tell you about?

A stagecoach about to depart in 1747.

Letters: railway transport

Read these three letters before answering the questions on page 30.

SOURCE 5g

(William Hedley to Dr Lardner, 1836. A copy was also sent to the *Courant* newspaper for publication)

In your highly-popular Lectures you stated that Mr Stephenson was the Father of the Locomotive Engine. Now, I do not wish to detract one iota from the Celebrity to which Mr Stephenson is entitled, – he has done much for the Locomotive Engine; but, by referring to Mr Wood's Book on Railroads . . . it appears that a Locomotive Engine was not constructed by Mr S. before 25th July, 1814. Long before this Period the Use of Horses on the Wylam Railroad was superceded by the Locomotive Engines, and a large annual Sum in the course of being saved to the Colliery from the reduced Charge in conveying the Coals. My Patent bears the Date 13th March, 1813.

In Conclusion, I beg to say, that I am the person who established the Principle of Locomotion by the Friction or Adhesion of the Wheels upon the Rails; and further, that it was the Engines on the Wylam Railroad that established the Character of the Locomotive Engine in this District, as an efficient and . . . economical prime Mover. After this statement . . . I trust you will see the Propriety in your future Lectures of not designating Mr Stephenson the 'Father of the Locomotive Engine'.

I beg to subscribe myself, Sir,
Your obedient servant,

WM HEDLEY.

SOURCE 5h

(George Stephenson to Edward Pease, 1821)

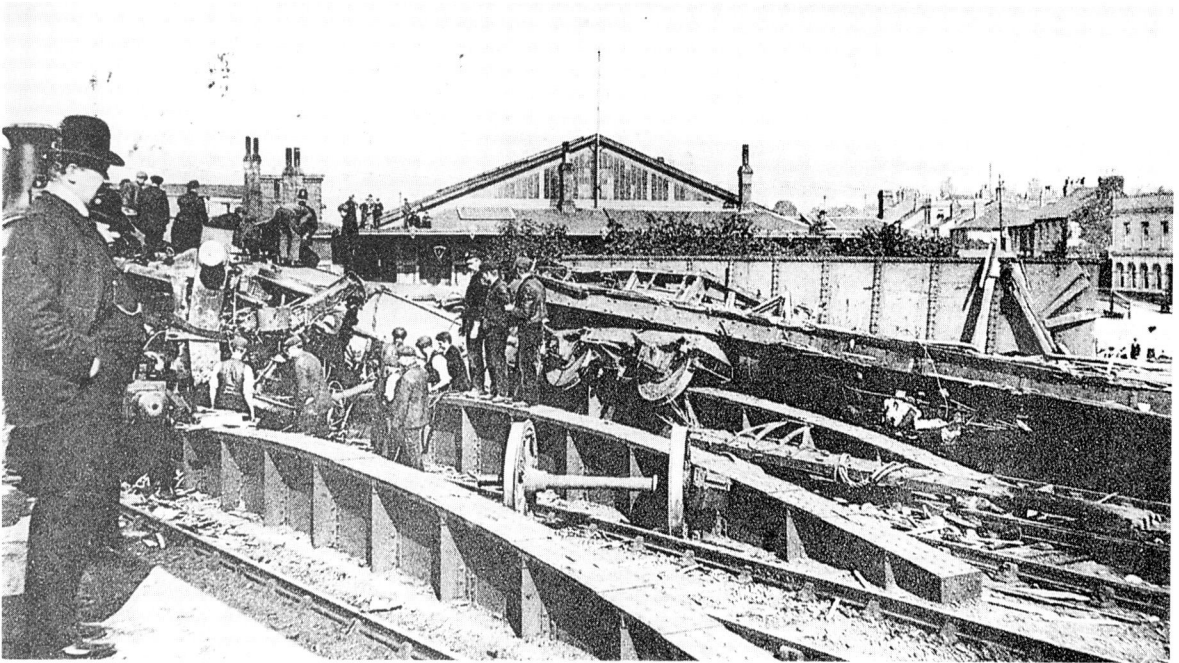

A railway accident at Salisbury Station in 1906. Twenty-seven people died.

SOURCE 5i

(Charles Dickens to Thomas Mitton, 1865. He is describing a railway accident on the South Eastern Railway. Ten people were killed)

My Dear Mitton,

I should have written to you yesterday or the day before, if I had been quite up to writing.

I was in the only carriage that did not go over into the stream. It was caught upon the turn by some of the ruin of the bridge, and hung suspended and balanced in an apparently impossible manner. Two ladies were my fellow-passengers, an old one and a young one . . . The old lady cried out 'My God!' and the young one screamed. I caught hold of them both . . . and said: 'We can't help ourselves, but we can be quiet and composed. Pray don't cry out.' The old lady immediately answered: 'Thank you. Rely upon me. Upon my soul I will be quiet.' . . .

I got out with great caution and stood upon the step. Some people in the two other compartments were madly trying to plunge out of the window, and had no idea that there was an open swampy field fifteen feet down below them, and nothing else! The two guards (one with his face cut) were running up and down on the down side of the bridge quite wildly. I called out to them: 'Look at me. Do stop an instant and look at me, and tell me whether you don't know me.' One of them answered, 'We know you very well, Mr Dickens.' 'Then,' I said, 'my good fellow, for God's sake give me your key, and send one of those labourers here, and I'll empty this carriage.' . . .

Suddenly I came upon a staggering man covered with blood (I think he must have been flung clean out of his carriage), with such a frightful cut across the skull that I couldn't bear to look at him. I poured some water over his face and gave him some drink, then gave him some brandy, and laid him down on the grass, and he said: 'I am gone,' and died afterwards . . .

I don't want to be examined at the inquest and I don't want to write about it. I could do no good either way, and I could only seem to speak about myself, which of course I would rather not do. I am keeping very quiet here. I have a – I don't know what to call it – constitutional (I suppose) presence of mind, and was not in the least fluttered at the time . . .

Ever faithfully,

Charles Dickens.

EXERCISES

1 Using a whole page, copy out the chart below. Answer the questions about each source in the spaces provided.

2 Using the information on your chart, write a summary explaining how *useful* and *reliable* you consider these three letters are.

SOURCE	PURPOSE and CIRCUMSTANCES When and where was it written? And why?	AUDIENCE Who was the letter for?	What view does the author give of himself?	INFORMATION What does the source particularly tell us about?	INADEQUACIES What does the source especially *fail* to tell us about?
5g					
5h					
5i					

Autobiographies

When important people write the story of their lives, their autobiographies are of great value to historians. They include more details of events than general books. They have stories and comments about other people who played a part in events.

So historians are able to gain a better understanding of the motives of people and of the discussions which went on. The different points of view of those involved will be identified. In the end, a more detailed and accurate picture of why things happened as they did is likely to emerge.

On the other hand, autobiographies must be treated with caution. They are not always written by the actual people. The famous case of Robert Blincoe, in the box opposite, is just one example of this.

Even if the subjects have written their own stories, it may be that they were written deliberately to show off their part in events. However, this does not mean that all autobiographies are written for this purpose and will *necessarily* be biased. The first extract which follows is from the autobiography of William Adams. He wrote his life story when he was nearly 70 years old. His schooldays began at a **dame school**. In his autobiography, he admitted that he only remembered this because the old lady shook him so much that he was ill.

In this extract, he describes a later experience of another fee-paying school.

SOURCE 5j

(W E Adams: *Memoirs of a Social Atom*, 1903. The author was a leading working-class **radical** and a supporter of **Chartism**)

The only two schools for poor children were situated too far away to be available in my case. So I was sent to one of the few private [schools] that then flourished in the town. It was known as Gardner's Academy.

The proprietor of this establishment was Joseph Aldan Gardner – a fiddler and dancing-master as well as a teacher of youth. Mr Gardner had one distinct qualification for the office he had assumed. He was a clever penman – the cleverest I have ever known. Writing was almost the only accomplishment I acquired under his tuition.

But the schoolmaster at one time occupied, in

In 1828, a thin volume was published. It claimed to tell the story of a man called Robert Blincoe. It was the story of his days as an apprentice in the cotton industry. Most textbooks quote it when describing working conditions in the early mills.

However, it was published in strange circumstances. Although it is called *A Memoir*, it was not written by Blincoe. Blincoe told his story to Brown, who acted rather like a **ghost-writer**.

It was first published in 1828, when Brown himself was dead. (He had committed suicide.) Blincoe did not know it was being published. It was reprinted in 1832, just before the Government set up an enquiry into factory conditions.

The **propaganda** value of the book was obvious to those who wanted to see conditions improved. The title-page of the 1832 print (on the right) made that very clear. Details in the book, such as beatings of young children, supported what witnesses told the enquiry.

A historian therefore needs to ask:
- why was the book written?
- why was it published?
- what other evidence supports what is written in the autobiography?

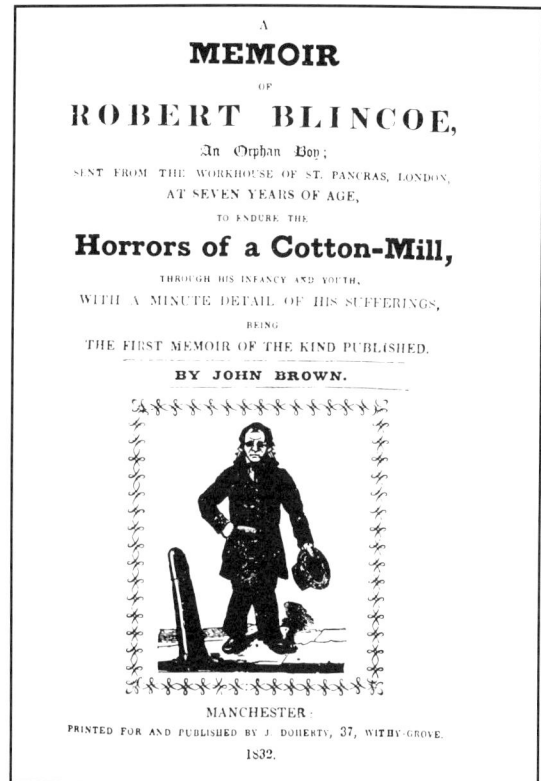

A
MEMOIR
OF
ROBERT BLINCOE,
An Orphan Boy;
SENT FROM THE WORKHOUSE OF ST. PANCRAS, LONDON,
AT SEVEN YEARS OF AGE,
TO ENDURE THE
Horrors of a Cotton-Mill,
THROUGH HIS INFANCY AND YOUTH,
WITH A MINUTE DETAIL OF HIS SUFFERINGS,
BEING
THE FIRST MEMOIR OF THE KIND PUBLISHED.
BY JOHN BROWN.

MANCHESTER:
PRINTED FOR AND PUBLISHED BY J. DOHERTY, 37, WITHY-GROVE.
1832.

the estimation of his boys, a secondary place in his own academy. The first place was then held by a tame magpie, which performed the twofold duty of diverting the scholars and making an intolerable mess of benches, desks, and copy-books. It need hardly be said that the education imparted ... was not of the highest ... quality.

Most of the scholars, however, fared much better than I did. The difference arose in this way. My dear old grandmother was too poor to pay even the small fee required – sixpence or eighteenpence a week [2½ – 3 p]. It was therefore agreed that she and her daughters should do an equivalent amount of laundry-work for the schoolmaster and his family. The arrangement was not satisfactory so far as I was concerned. Looked upon as belonging to a lower social grade than the boys who paid for their schooling in cash, I received much less attention than the other scholars. I learnt how to read and write – that was all.

EXERCISES

1 (a) What can you learn about nineteenth century education from this account?
(b) Does this mean that all schools were like this? Explain your answer.
2 (a) Why did Adams feel that he 'received much less attention than the other scholars'?
(b) What evidence does he give that he received less attention? (Think carefully.)
3 Read the introduction to this source. Why should a historian treat this source with care?

SOURCE 5k

(H W Harding: 'Bunts for the oven – and a saw to cut the salt.' This article was published in the *Hampshire Magazine*, 1973)

I was born in Ropley in March, 1884, at the

General Stores in Gilbert Street, and have lived in Ropley all my life, except for a period of nearly four years in the first world war.

My grandparents had a shop in Cheriton, and wanted a branch shop; when my grandfather had the opportunity of getting possession of the Ropley shop, he sent my parents to manage it. I went to Ropley School at about five years of age and left at thirteen to learn to weigh and pack groceries.

Everything came in large quantities – sugar in two cwt bags, soda in the same, flour in two-and-a-half cwt sacks, currants and raisins in 56 lb boxes. The latter had to be put through a sieve and cleaned. We ground coffee for customers.

Salt came by rail, a truck of five tons, which was parked in a store at the back of the two bread ovens. We had a special saw with which to cut penny blocks. We also sold meal and corn and the like.

When I was about sixteen I started work in the bakehouse. Everything in the making of bread was done by hand. What was called 'stirring a sponge' was done overnight: a small quantity of flour was put in the very long trough, then a pen-board was inserted to hold it in the front end of the trough and yeast and a pail of water added. In the morning, salt was added and water, according to the quantity of bread required for the day.

We had two horses and carts and two men to work in the bakehouse and deliver bread and groceries; mother paid a small licence to enable her to drive to Alresford.

Our two ovens were heated with bunts – copse wood about three feet in length, with a few thicker sticks. We bought bunts by the thousand, and they were stacked like hayricks.

On Sundays some of the neighbours brought their Sunday dinners and cakes to be cooked. By this time, my two brothers had come home from learning the trade. We then had three more horses and carts and several young men to work up more rounds.

We also killed and cured our own bacon and pork. Some cottagers kept two pigs, and we supplied them with meal and middlings; when they were ready, we had one to offset the account. All of our customers had a pound of currants and raisins and a large calendar for Christmas. There was no early closing day; later on, we closed at six, and later still at one. We had our first motor van, an old Ford, in 1920.

The shophouse where I was born has been demolished for road-widening.

The family outside the General Stores. The author is on the right.

EXERCISES

4 What aspects of life does Harding provide information about?
5 Why do you think people took their food to the shop to be cooked on Sundays?
6 (a) What changes does the author describe in shop life?
   (b) Does this mean there were no other changes? Explain your answer.
7 How *useful* and *reliable* are these two sources, in your opinion?

Biographies

Biographies have many of the same advantages as autobiographies. Their authors will have researched their subjects carefully. They will have studied as many as possible of the available documents and papers, including diaries and letters. If possible, they will have interviewed people who knew the subject and may even have spent time with the subjects themselves.

The books that result will give a very full picture of a person. So, like autobiographies, they should help historians to answer these questions:

- What happened?
- Why did it happen?
- What did people think and feel about it?

However, biographies do have disadvantages. The authors may not have been able to get at all the information they wanted. They may wish to show their subjects in a very favourable or unfavourable light. If so, the biography will be biased.

Authors will obviously want people to buy their books so they try to make them interesting and appealing. They might have to leave out some details to do this. They might make some things sound a bit more exciting than they really were.

You may find several biographies that give a different view of the same person. In the following exercise, you will examine different opinions about Florence Nightingale.

SOURCE 5l

(Joe Scott: *Medicine Through Time*, 1987)

Florence Nightingale was born in 1820. Her parents were rich, and she and her elder sister were educated at home by governesses and by their father. Florence was intelligent, lively and attractive, and it seemed as if she would soon find a husband – the only acceptable future for a girl of the English upper classes at the time.

But Florence turned down several very eligible young men, and determined to devote her life to a higher purpose . . .

Her parents were horrified [with her plans] and it took her seven years to persuade them to agree. She quarrelled bitterly with her mother and elder sister over this, but her father gave her some support, and in 1851 she was allowed to go for training to Kaiserwerth in Germany.

SOURCE 5m

(R W Pirton: *A Pageant of History*, 1962)

Every day she worked, thinking nothing of herself, and the nurses who were with her worked equally unselfishly, nursing the injured, helping them to write letters home if they were unable to do so themselves, speaking words of comfort to those who had particular problems.

SOURCE 5n

(M R S Andrews: *The Soldiers' Angel* in *Great Lives, Great Deeds*, 1965)

Today, a figure of Florence Nightingale stands, lofty, on a pedestal in London. That is as it should be; but it is not all. Her truest monument, not made with hands, is one not always associated with her name; it is the far-reaching outcome of that school of thirteen young women in brown and white, housed and guarded in a wing of old St Thomas's Hospital. It is the hope of help to which the world turns in trouble, a fitting, enormous monument – the modern profession of nursing.

SOURCE 5o

(*The Macmillan Encyclopaedia*, 1987)

Nightingale, Florence (1820–1910). British hospital reformer and founder of the nursing profession. With strong religious convictions, Florence Nightingale trained as a nurse and was appointed as a nursing superintendent in London in 1853.

On the outbreak of the Crimean War in 1854, she volunteered to lead a party of nurses to work in the military hospitals. She set about transforming the appalling conditions, earning herself the title *Lady with the Lamp* from the patients.

After the war, she was instrumental in obtaining improved conditions in the army and, in 1860, from a Nightingale Fund, subscribed by the public, she established a Nightingale School for Nurses at St Thomas's Hospital – the first of its kind. In 1907 Florence Nightingale became the first woman to receive the OM (Order of Merit).

Florence Nightingale looking after the sick.

EXERCISES

1 (a) Which of the written and visual sources gives a favourable view of Florence Nightingale?
(b) Which of the written and visual sources gives an unfavourable impression of her?
   In each case, explain how you decided, quoting from the sources, where appropriate.
2 Do any of the sources give you any clues about *why* she undertook the work that she did, rather than just telling you what she did? Explain your answer.
3 There are very few sources that are critical of Florence Nightingale. Do you think this is because:
(a) She has become a heroine in British history, and any historian who criticised her would be unpopular
(b) even if there was anything for which she might be criticised, the results of her work were so good that these can be ignored
(c) she really was a perfect, saintly person?
   Explain why you have chosen or rejected each of these explanations.
4 Are biographies which only praise their subjects of any value to historians? Give reasons for your answer.
5 Study Source 5p below. In what ways, and why, is Strachey's view of Florence Nightingale different to the others? Explain your answer.

SOURCE 5p

(Lytton Strachey: *Eminent Victorians*, 1918)

Certainly, she was heroic. Yet her heroism was not of that simple sort so dear to the readers of novels . . . the romantic sentimental heroism with which mankind loves to invest its chosen darlings: it was made of sterner stuff.

To the wounded soldier on his couch of agony she might well appear in the guise of a gracious angel of mercy; but the military surgeons, and the orderlies, and her own nurses . . . could tell a different story. It was not by gentle sweetness and womanly [self-denial] that she had brought order out of chaos in the Scutari Hospitals, that, from her own resources, she had clothed the British Army, that she had spread her dominion over the . . . reluctant powers of the official world; it was by strict method, by stern discipline, by rigid attention to detail, by ceaseless labour, by the fixed determination of an [unconquerable] will.

Beneath her cool and calm [manner] lurked fierce and passionate fires. As she passed through the wards in her plain dress, so quiet, so unassuming, she struck the casual observer simply as . . . a perfect lady; but the keener eye [saw] something more than that – . . . the sign of power in the curve of the thin nose, and the traces of a harsh and dangerous temper – something mocking, and yet something precise – in the small and delicate mouth.

A cartoonist's view of Florence Nightingale at work in the Crimean War.

—6—
Newspapers

Newspapers are a rich source of information for historians. News stories tell us what happened and the **editorials** and letters give us views and opinions on these events. The advertisements, features and radio programme lists also give a later generation an idea of what life was like at a particular time.

The newspaper advertisements shown on these pages are all taken from the turn of the century. Study them carefully before answering the questions.

EXERCISES

1 (a) Whom was each advert aimed at? Explain how you decided.
(b) From the Hackney Furnishing advert what can you learn about (i) heating and (ii) beds at that time?
(c) From the Goddard's advert, what can you learn about the jobs of male and female servants?
2 How do they differ in *style* from modern newspaper adverts?
3 Are any of the products they are advertising still commonly sold today? Explain your answer.
4 Choose any subject related to social and economic issues today, such as transport or the environment. For one week, make a collection of newspaper cuttings about your topic. Try to do this using two different papers.

At the end of the week, put your collection together. Then use your sources to write a summary of what has happened that week. (Write about 250 words). Finally, explain in what ways your two sources differed in their coverage of the topic.

'A Boon to Women' – the electric corset, advertised in the Thame Gazette, 1892.

5 In groups, compare at least two modern newspapers (or one modern and one old one). Analyse the different types of information included, such as:

- national news
- letters
- editorial comments
- sport
- TV and radio programmes
- advertisements

You should do this by counting up how many column centimetres are used on each category. Then draw up graphs to illustrate the different types. Finally, write a report on your findings, and evaluate the papers you have studied.

A nineteenth century advertisement for Goddard's cleaners, showing who did what.

Furnishings for a 'working-man's home' for £14.25, advertised in the News of the World, *1910.*

Although newspapers can be of great value to historians, they must also be treated with care. One problem is that they are trying to report news quickly. So they sometimes make mistakes, as Sources 6a and 6b below illustrate.

SOURCE 6a

(*The Daily Telegraph*, October 22 1988)

Freighter rammed us, say owners

British children leap into sea as cruise ship sinks

All 475 school party members are safe, says Greek embassy

By Our Foreign Staff

A GREEK cruise ship carrying 475 British children and teachers on a Mediterranean cruise sank last night after a collision with an Italian cargo ship about a mile outside the port of Piraeus. But four hours after the collision fears of heavy casualties were allayed when a spokesman at the British Embassy in Athens said all the children had been rescued.

SOURCE 6b

(*The Sunday Telegraph*, October 23 1988)

Cruise Children fly to reunion

The parents of 14-year-old Vivienne Barley, the one British girl missing after the sinking of the cruise ship Jupiter, were clinging to hope that she was still alive last night as hundreds of survivors flew home to tearful reunions with their parents.

But Greek authorities said Vivienne was missing, presumed drowned . . .

Vivienne, from Walsall in the West Midlands, appeared to be the only Briton missing after the sinking. Her father, Mr

Richard Barley, a motorcycle policeman, said he and his wife, Janet, at first thought they had seen her on a television news bulletin, coming ashore . . .

Mr and Mrs Barley . . . went to bed certain that their daughter had been saved. Then, at 3 am, they received a telephone call from a Foreign Office official to say she was the only pupil who had not been traced.

Newspapers often support a particular party or point of view. They will try to show that viewpoint in a good light. So they may report events in a subjective way.

This can easily be done by selecting what information to include, or stressing some facts rather than others. Another technique is to use emotive language to stir up the reader's feelings.

In 1819, people gathered at St Peter's Field in Manchester. The occasion was a meeting to demand the reform of Parliament. The magistrates said the meeting was illegal and decided to arrest the speakers. The most famous of these was Henry Hunt, nicknamed 'Orator'.

The next two sources describe what happened next – an event often called *The Peterloo Massacre*.

SOURCE 6c

(The *Manchester Mercury*, 17 August, 1819)

The events of yesterday will bring down upon the name of Hunt, and his accomplices, the deep and lasting **execrations** of many a sorrowing family, and of the well-affected members of society at large . . . Having daringly invited the attendance of a mass of people, which . . . may . . . be computed at 100 000 individuals, they proceeded to address them with language and suggestions of the usual desperate and **malevolent** character . . .

[Just before two o'clock] the bugle sounded, and the Manchester and Salford Yeomanry Cavalry, who . . . had been in attendance about ten minutes, advanced in full charge through the multitude, and surrounded the **Orators** upon their own stage . . .

Now ensues a most painful and melancholy part of our recital: the necessary ardour of the troops in the discharge of their duty has led, we lament to say, to some fatal and many serious accidents. A respectable innkeeper who was . . . a special constable, was rode over and mortally wounded; another young man, who is at present unknown, experienced the same fate.

SOURCE 6d

(*The Times*, August 19 1819)

. . . the Manchester Yeomanry Cavalry rode into the mob which gave way before them and directed their course to the cart from which Hunt was speaking. Not a brickbat was thrown at them – not a pistol was fired during this period: all was quiet and orderly, as if the cavalry had been the friends of the multitude, and had marched as such into the midst of them . . .

[At this point, Hunt is arrested.]

As soon as Hunt had jumped from the waggon, a cry was made by the cavalry, 'Have at their flags.' In consequence, they immediately dashed not only at the flags which were in the waggon, but those which were posted among the crowd, cutting most indiscriminately to the right and to the left in order to get at them.

This set the people running in all directions, and it was not till this act had been committed that any brick-bats were hurled at the military. From that moment the Manchester Yeomanry Cavalry lost all command of temper.

A person of the name of Saxton . . . was standing in the cart. Two privates rode up to him. 'There,' said one of them, 'is that villain, Saxton; do you run him through the body.' 'No,' replied the other, 'I had rather not – I leave it to you.'

The man immediately made a lunge at Saxton, and it was only by slipping aside that the blow missed his life. As it was, it cut his coat and waistcoat, but fortunately did him no other injury. A man within five yards of us in another direction had his nose completely taken off by a blow of a **sabre** . . .

Seeing all this hideous work going on, we felt an alarm which any man may be forgiven for feeling in a similar situation: looking around, we saw a constable at no great distance, and . . . appealed to him for assistance. He immediately took us into custody, and on our saying that we merely attended to report the proceedings of the day, he replied, 'Oh! Oh! You then are one of their writers – you must go before the magistrates.'

This cartoon shows the yeomanry in action at the 'massacre' of Peterloo in 1819.

Massacre at St Peters or "BRITONS STRIKE HOME"!!!

6 (a) What view of (i) the crowd and (ii) the soldiers does *The Manchester Mercury* take? Write down the words or phrases that led to your decision.
(b) Now, answer the same question about *The Times* story.

7 (a) Why do you think two reporters took different views of this event?
(b) Does this mean that one of them was wrong? Explain your answer.

8 Are Sources 6c and 6d biased? Give reasons.

9 How useful and reliable do you think each of these sources is?

Newspapers are keen to sell as many copies as they can. So they sometimes choose stories that they think will appeal to their readers.

They may also try to report the stories in an exciting or exaggerated way. As a result, it is difficult to judge what value to place on an article, both as a source of information and as a guide to opinions at the time.

SOURCE 6e

(*Sunday Sport*, November 13 1988)

Green-fingered aliens shocker

Shocked gran Jean Coolsting told last night how green-fingered aliens beamed down to work on her garden.

Jean, 62, says a blazing UFO hovered outside her bedroom windows and sprayed intergalactic fertiliser over her flowers and trimmed her favourite dahlias.

'I got up in the morning and there was a strange, mist-like liquid all over the lawn and bushes,' said the hospital worker from Camberley, Surrey.

'As far as I know, it was a deposit from a spaceship and, believe it or not, this has happened before.

'Our family must attract them . . . we've had 20 UFO sightings between us.

'On the visit in question they had a strange effect on the greenery. It helped the flowers grow.'

In some cases, reporters will write stories that seem to be factual accounts, but actually contain their own opinions. At other times, reporters will quote from eyewitnesses.

But these people may be in a state of shock and may not have seen the whole of an event. Even then, reporters will have to cut down their interviews to just a few lines, and will pick what to use and what to leave out.

During times of crisis, newspapers are interesting, but dangerous, sources. Papers are often **censored** at these times, with the editors only being allowed to publish what the government says they can.

The General Strike

Bias in newspapers can be seen most clearly during the General Strike of 1926. Indeed, one newspaper actually helped to cause the strike. Printers at the *Daily Mail* refused to print the issue of May 3.

They objected to its editorial, titled 'For King and Country'. This compared the threat of a General Strike with a foreign war. It asked 'all law-abiding men and women' to stand out against a 'revolutionary movement'.

By Tuesday May 4, the **TUC** had called out all printers on strike. The newspaper owners had to produce their papers as best they could. Newspapers continued to appear – but they were much smaller than usual.

The government issued its own paper, called the *British Gazette* and edited by Winston Churchill. It was open propaganda and many politicians did not like it. Churchill saw his job as doing anything he could to break the strike.

The TUC published the *British Worker*, calling it the 'Official Strike News Bulletin'. The government at first tried to stop it, then tried to stop it getting paper to print on.

Read the three newspaper extracts which follow. They were taken from the *British Gazette*, the *British Worker* and the *Daily Express*.

10 (a) Which source do you think came from which newspaper? Explain how you decided.
(b) Do you think the *Daily Express* supported the government or the workers? Give a reason for your choice.

11 (a) Take each source in turn. Write down any examples of bias in the source.
(b) Does this mean that the source is of no value to historians? Give reasons.

12 Write a news item for the government paper based on Source 6g. Remember that the headline is an important part of the item.

13 Look at the two photographs from the General Strike.
(a) You are the editor of the *British Worker*. Write captions for these photographs.

Students took over from dock workers on strike.

(b) You are Winston Churchill. Write captions for them to appear in the *British Gazette*.
(c) What does this exercise tell you about the problems of newspapers as primary sources?

SOURCE 6f

(May 10)

ALL'S WELL!

The General Council's Message to Trade Union Members

We are entering upon the second week of the general stoppage in support of the mine workers against the attack upon their standard of life by the coalowners.

Nothing could be more wonderful than the magnificent response of millions of workers to the call of their leaders.

From every town and city in the country, reports are pouring into the General Council headquarters stating that all ranks are solid, that the working men and women are resolute in their determination to resist the unjust attack upon the mining community.

(May 11)

Surprising London

'Business as usual'.
Americans are Astonished

Visitors from the Continent who arrived in London over the week-end expressed their astonishment; they expected to find difficulties in getting to London, but the Continental train service is nearly normal. There are plenty of porters at the railway stations and more and more trains every day . . .

A group of Americans [in the Strand] could hardly believe their eyes. They had left Paris for a great adventure, expecting to find the 'gloom' an American newspaper had reported. Instead they saw London going about its business as usual. Except that most of the omnibuses carried a policeman, the Americans could find nothing unusual.

(May 12)

ORDER AND QUIET THROUGH THE LAND
Growing Dissatisfaction Among The Strikers

INCREASING NUMBERS OF MEN RETURNING TO WORK
850 Omnibuses In The Streets of London

MORE AND MORE TRAINS
—————— *Whitehall, May 11.* ——————

The situation throughout the country shows further improvement.

The distribution of food supplies gives no cause whatever for apprehension. There have been a few reports of temporary local shortage in particular [goods], but on investigation it has been found that [most] of these reports are inaccurate. In the remaining cases the necessary steps have been at once taken to make the position secure. Especially large supplies of sugar were distributed yesterday . . .

Sharp sentences have been imposed by the local magistrates on a number of persons who were arrested last week for disorder and **intimidation** . . .

It can be . . . definitely stated that there is a growing dissatisfaction among the strikers with the policy of a General Strike, and considerable uneasiness as to its ultimate results.

A rare example of violence during the General Strike. This car was a casualty in the East End of London.

—7—
Cartoons

Cartoons are always entertaining and this makes them an attractive way of presenting history. Their impact helps us to remember things that might otherwise soon be forgotten. Most of us enjoy comic strips when we are young, and cartoons are an extension of these. They make our usually serious leaders look rather silly, and exaggerate their funniest characteristics.

There are large quantities of cartoons available for the study of the period from 1750. The magazine *Punch* has been published since 1841, and many famous nineteenth century cartoons first appeared in it.

However, it is not always easy to use these cartoons as historical sources. Many were extremely detailed and had lengthy **captions** that are hard to understand. And, today, some of them no longer seem funny.

A particular problem is that cartoons do not usually tell us what happened. They are to make us laugh at someone or something. But cartoons are drawn to make people laugh *at the time*. So they rely on a lot of knowledge about what was actually happening at that time. The cartoon opposite is a good example. It was printed in *Private Eye* in 1962.

To understand it, you need to know:

1 The man on the left is a doctor.

2 Thalidomide was a drug which was on sale in the early 1960s as a tranquilliser.
3 It had a serious side-effect: if taken by pregnant women, it could cause deformed children.
4 'The illegal operation' which the woman is suggesting is an **abortion**. Abortions were illegal until 1967.

This cartoon is not trying to make us laugh out loud. It is showing the irony in the situation. The woman has been given a drug which can deform babies. Yet she cannot get an abortion to end her pregnancy. So the baby will be born deformed.

trog

I'm sorry but the ethical position is quite clear. Thalidomide was a legal prescription, but what you suggest is an illegal operation.

On these pages are two cartoons from *Punch*, together with another commenting on women's fashions. Study them carefully, and then answer these questions as fully as possible.

1 (a) What has happened in Source 7a?
 (b) Is the man embarrassed or amused? Explain how you decided.

2 Source 7b is an early comment on women campaigning for women's rights. How do you think people at the time would have reacted to it?

3 (a) How were men expected to react to Source 7c in 1894?
 (b) Do you think these cartoons were drawn by men or women? Give reasons for your view.

4 Compare the style and sense of humour in these cartoons with those of modern cartoons.

5 What do these cartoons tell you about attitudes to women in the nineteenth century?

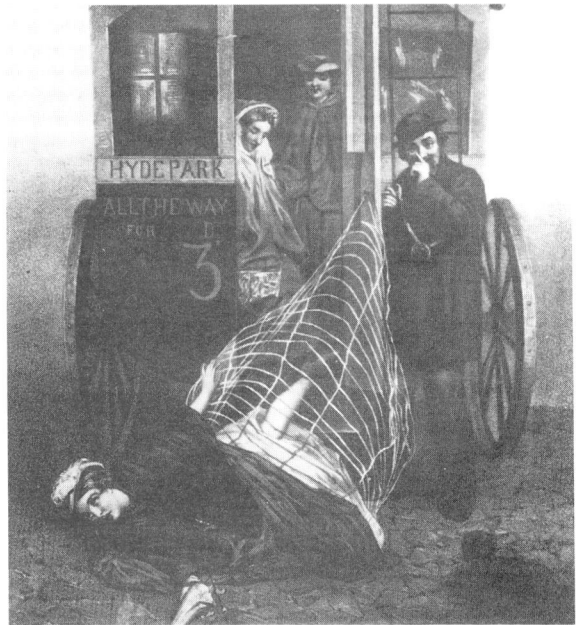

SOURCE 7b

(From *Punch*, 1882)

HER RIGHTS.

Old Gent (mildly). "PRAY, ARE YOU AN ADVOCATE OF WOMAN'S RIGHTS, MA'AM?"
Lady (sharply). "MOST CERTAINLY I AM, SIR. WHY DO YOU ASK?"
Old Gent. "BECAUSE I WAS ABOUT TO OFFER YOU MY SEAT; BUT OF COURSE YOU CLAIM THE RIGHT TO STAND!"

(From *Punch*, 1894)

(Government poster of the second world war)

THE 'NEW WOMAN'

The Vicar's Wife. *'And have you had good sport, Miss Goldenberg!'*

Miss G. *'Oh, Rippin'! I only shot one rabbit, but I managed to injure quite a dozen more!'*

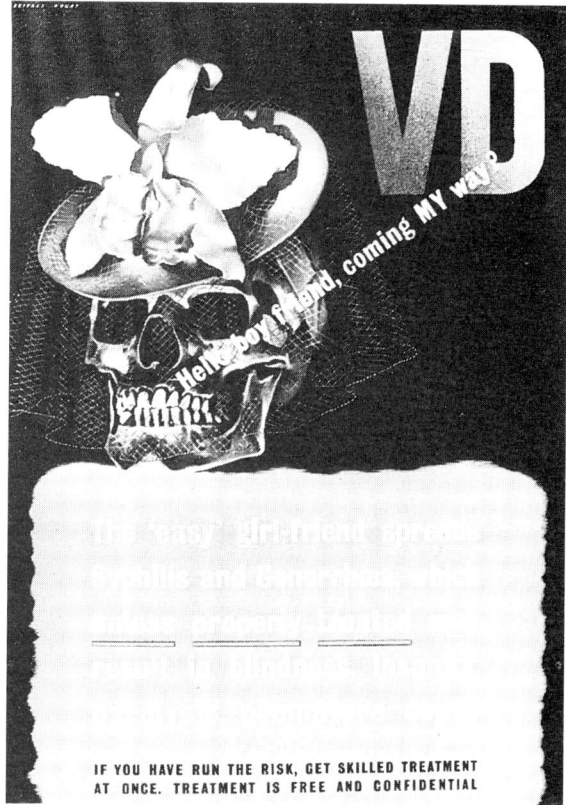

IF YOU HAVE RUN THE RISK, GET SKILLED TREATMENT AT ONCE. TREATMENT IS FREE AND CONFIDENTIAL

It is not only newspapers and magazines which publish cartoons. Often, governments use them to put across a particular point or further a campaign, like that about Aids in the late twentieth century.

In the second world war, the government was especially concerned about the spread of **venereal diseases** among soldiers. Its cartoon advertising campaign, an example of which is shown in Source 7d, pulled no punches. Compare this with a modern Aids warning. Which is more frightening?

EXERCISE

6 Draw a line down the centre of a page. Head one half: *The value of cartoons as historical evidence*, and the other half: *The problems of using cartoons*. Then write down as many things as you can under each heading. Try to include references to the cartoons in this chapter as you do so. Here are two to help you start – you have to choose which column to put them in:

● they are amusing and easy to remember, like the lady falling off the back of the bus.

● their sense of humour is not necessarily funny to a later generation, like the comment on women shooting rabbits.

—8—
Pictures

Until the invention of photography, drawings and paintings were important ways of recording events. Today, they are only important in circumstances where photography is not possible.

You may have seen on television an artist's drawings of the scene inside a courtroom. This is because cameras are not allowed inside British courts.

So it would seem that pictures are going to be very useful to a historian studying events until about 1850. However, by now you will have guessed that no kind of historical source is without its problems.

Pictures pose problems because the artists were not trying to make historical sources for people to study years later. They were producing works of art. Their paintings may have been made for sale; their drawings might have been used to illustrate books. Either way, the artist had to make a living. If people did not like the pictures, he or she would not be offered more work.

So the first question to ask is:
- why was the picture made?

Look at the picture of Queen Victoria in 1837. This was drawn in a book published in 1887. It was the 50th anniversary of her coronation. People were very proud of their queen. They would expect to see her looking her best.

So the artist shows her looking at her best – perhaps even slightly better than her best. Portrait pictures were usually made to flatter the person being painted. Very often, he or she was actually paying for the picture. Study the section in the box on the opposite page on James Brindley.

SOURCE 8a

James Brindley was born in 1716; as a young man, he could not read or write. He was a labourer who became an apprentice at the age of 17, later becoming a millwright. His work on the Bridgewater Canal made him famous – and rich. By the time this portrait was painted, he was a gentleman. Note the cut of his clothes. He can afford to look self-satisfied as he looks out on the world.

The next question to ask is:
● where was the picture going to appear?
Unfortunately, textbooks rarely answer this question for you. Yet it is important to know. The next picture shows factory children scavenging for food in a pig trough.

Look at the children's clothing. They have no shoes. They are eating whatever they can get their hands on. It seems to tell us a lot about the conditions in which these children worked.

Textbooks often use this picture to illustrate chapters on factory conditions. What they don't always say is that it actually comes from a novel published in the first half of the nineteenth century. It is illustrating a scene from the book. It is possible that the artist never went near a factory in his life.

So the next question to ask is:
● did the artist actually see what he or she has drawn?
Often, we have to guess this. On the next page, look at the famous picture of the Barton Aqueduct on the Bridgewater Canal. It was knocked down in the 1890s,

a The Duke of Bridgewaters. Navigation a Cross the Irwell b Barton Bridge over J c

An early print of Barton Aqueduct.

This photograph shows Barton Aqueduct in the distance. Soon afterwards, it was pulled down to make way for the Manchester Ship Canal.

when the Manchester Ship Canal was built. So photographs of it are not very common.

However, the blurred photograph below does prove that the artist got the proportions of the bridge right. But what about the boat?

The boat in the drawing is a sailing boat. Yet it is pulled by a horse walking along the towpath. Notice where the rope is attached. What happens when the horse pulls? Did the artist really see this scene or has he used his imagination to make the picture more attractive?

Of course, any artist would want to make his or her picture appealing. That does not mean it must look pretty. The picture of children carrying clay in a brickyard (opposite) was almost certainly trying to make people feel sorry for the children.

But look at the girl in the centre. Her clothes are tattered and she has no shoes but notice how clean she looks. She is the only one looking straight at you, as you look at the picture. Has the artist tried to make her look attractive? Some people think so.

Child workers in a brickyard.

EXERCISES

1 (a) Why is it difficult to find portraits of famous people that are accurate and true-to-life?
  (b) Even if they are not accurate, what can a historian learn from them?
2 (a) Why does the picture of the children scavenging for food often appear in textbooks?
  (b) Is it justified for authors to use it in this way?
3 Why might the artist of Source 8f have made one girl look attractive?
4 (a) Do the problems associated with pictures as evidence make them worthless as historical sources?
  (b) What are the advantages of pictures to historians?

Pictures as propaganda

Pictures have a much greater impact than words. People were well aware of that in the eighteenth and nineteenth centuries. The Mines Report of 1842 was unusual because it included woodcut pictures of work underground, and of the miners themselves. Most of the pictures showing mining conditions underground in the early nineteenth century come from this report.

The picture below is from the report. It shows a mining woman naked to the waist. This was normal underground because of the heat. But people were actually more shocked by the moral risk to women and young girls than by the fact that they were working at all.

The reformers knew this well. Half-clothed female miners were more likely to get MPs to vote against women working underground than any number of facts about the effect of the work.

SOURCE 8g

The Mines Report of 1842 included this picture of a girl miner, naked to the waist. Textbooks usually use a similar picture of a fully clothed woman. Yet it was this kind of picture which Lord Londonderry described to the House of Lords as 'scandalous and obscene'. They were, he said 'more calculated to excite the feelings than to enlighten the judgement'.

In the end, the best way to judge the reliability of a picture is to compare it with another one. Of course, this is not always possible. Sometimes one picture has been copied from another anyway.

SOURCE 8h

The Iron Forge, *a painting by Joseph Wright of Derby, 1779.*

SOURCE 8i (left)

Another view of a forge. This one was in Birmingham, 1844.

EXERCISES

5 Why, in 1842, were MPs more concerned by women working half-clothed in mines, than by the effects of their work on their health?

6 Compare Sources 8h and 8i.
   (a) Which of these sources do you think is most accurate? Explain how you decided.
   (b) Why did painters produce pictures that gave a romantic view of some industries?

—9—
Photographs and Films

Perhaps you think you're on safer ground here. After all, you've probably heard the saying, 'The camera never lies'. So photographs must be a reliable source of evidence.

Wrong.

Photographs pose all sorts of problems. The most basic one is: Is it really a photograph at all?

This postcard of the Municipal Gardens in Southport was sent by Ruth to her friend Ethel in 1906. It looks like a photograph of the scene. So it is – up to a point.

SOURCE 9a

The illuminations at Southport.

The people have been photographed, but the scene has mostly been drawn. This was a common technique at the time. It made photos seem more real.

Victorian cameras required good daylight in order to take good pictures. Until roll-film was introduced in 1889, film had to be exposed very slowly. Indoors, even with good lighting, a person had to sit very still for a long time for the photographer to take a good picture.

The photographer did have one way of achieving this. He used a prop called an iron maiden. This photograph shows Princess Alexandra posing with one.

SOURCE 9b

Princess Alexandra, wife of the Prince of Wales, later King Edward VII.

Pictures of people in the nineteenth century are very formal. They had to sit around too long to look natural.

SOURCE 9c

Very often, photographs tell us very little in themselves. Look at Source 9c. A policeman watches a woman run towards him with a pointed instrument.

Is she about to attack him? Why has she got such a big shopping bag? Why are some men taking photographs in the background? Of course, it's almost impossible to say, unless we have some more information.

Early Times printed this picture under the headline *Maggie Thatcher litter snatcher* in 1988. It shows Mrs Thatcher picking up litter in St James's Park in London as part of a new anti-litter campaign.

So that solves the mystery. Mrs Thatcher was picking up litter. This is what the *Early Times* story said:

SOURCE 9d

(*Early Times*, 1988)

Prime Minister, Margaret Thatcher took on the job of litter collector last week in St James's Park, as she did her bit to help keep Britain tidy.

Mrs Thatcher used a litter stick to pick up rubbish, that had been specially strewn by park keepers, to launch her campaign against litter bugs.

So we are looking at a real photograph of Mrs Thatcher. But the 'litter' she is collecting is not real litter. It was actually clean crisp packets which the park keepers threw down for her to pick up.

This is what journalists call a 'photo opportunity'. In other words, someone has arranged a good scene for them to photograph. How useful does that make it as evidence?

So it is often not easy to know what a photograph shows until we find out more about it. Photographs can be faked by photographers; they can be 'fixed' by other people.

In the same way, it is often very hard to say *when* a picture was taken. Look at this photo of the village of Downham in Lancashire. How do you work out when it was taken?

SOURCE 9e

An obvious start is to look at the roofs. There are no television aerials. You would expect some aerials if it was taken after about 1960.

But look closer and you will see there are no telephone wires either. That would suggest it is even older. You might guess 1920s or 1930s. You would be wrong.

In fact, the photo was taken in 1985. So why are there no TV aerials or telephone wires?

The answer is that the village is owned by Lord Clitheroe – and he doesn't want them. The people *do* have TV but there is just one aerial, hidden behind a barn. People get their TV pictures by underground cable. The telephone wires go underground, too. Lord Clitheroe wants to keep the village looking as it did years ago. So he paid to have the TV aerials removed.

There are, therefore, several ways in which photographs can be showing less than the truth. They might be partly drawn or painted. Early photographs could only show very still scenes or people. 'Photo opportunities' might have been arranged. The photograph might have been faked or set up, by the photographer or by someone else.

On the other hand, there are ways in which photographs can be helpful. Following the development of cameras in the 1840s and 1850s, there is an increasing stock of photographs of people, places and events in the nineteenth century.

For example, turnpikes are often thought of as an eighteenth-century development. Yet in many parts of the country, turnpikes were not built until later. Below is a photograph taken in 1860 which shows a uniformed turnpike keeper.

As with many other types of evidence, it tells us not only about the main subject (turnpikes) but also about other aspects of nineteenth-century life – clothes, houses and building materials, for example.

EXERCISES

1 Despite their disadvantages, what can historians learn from each of the Sources, 9a to 9f?
2 (a) Look at Source 9g on the next page. What does this photograph show?
   (b) Why is this photograph surprising?
   (c) What else does the photograph give you information about?
3 What can you learn from Source 9h?

SOURCE 9f

This is a real photograph of someone put in the stocks in 1855. The last known case was just ten years later.

SOURCE 9h

Mealtime at a teachers' training college in about 1905.

Photographs of ordinary people can also help us to understand better their feelings. This is especially true if they are used alongside other, written, sources.

4 In this chapter, several of the problems of using photographs have been examined.
(a) What do you consider the three main disadvantages of photos as historical evidence are?
(b) Given these disadvantages, are photos of *any* value as historical evidence? Explain your answer.

5 You will need to use other sources to do this question.
   Choose a topic associated with social or economic affairs today. Research photographs of your topic in newspapers, magazines and textbooks. If possible, take copies of them. Prepare and mount a display which includes a commentary on how the topic is presented in the photographs.

Films and television

There has been a huge increase in the number and quality of films in the last hundred years. From jerky black-and-white images, we have moved to high quality colour productions that can be stopped and started as the viewer pleases. On top of that, there are facilities for close-ups, replays and the like.
   There are many different kinds of films. Feature films are those that tell a story. Sometimes, they are based on historical themes or events. These can be very helpful in giving us a better understanding of the period and people.
   However, we have to be careful, as the story is rarely told exactly as it happened. The film maker's major task is to entertain, so he or she may have left parts out or changed things slightly to make the story more interesting. Sometimes, the story is based on a novel, then altered, such as the musical of *Oliver Twist*.

   Documentary films, cinema newsreels and government films all provide more direct forms of information, illustrated by

A 1948 version of Charles Dickens' Oliver Twist. *This scene shows mealtime in the workhouse. You could compare this with the impressions you gained from earlier sources about the Andover Workhouse. As a secondary source, is this helpful to a historian?*

suitable pictures. They can, therefore, give us a better knowledge and understanding than the written word, or radio.

However, these types of film are still made mainly to entertain, not to instruct. So they must be treated with care. For example, the **commentaries** on newsreels were always made to be interesting and exciting. They may not be strictly factual and may be biased.

Equally, not all the film that was shot will usually be used. Editors will have chosen what they want to be shown, so the problem of subjectivity by selection will occur.

'Information' films have also been used by governments for propaganda purposes. They can put across information about their plans and ideas in such a way that the audience will be impressed and accept the ideas they are hearing and seeing.

This sort of film is usually made for political purposes, but can be used for other reasons. In some ways, Sources 9i and 9j are examples of this.

Film, like any other form of evidence, needs to be treated very carefully. For each film, the historian needs to ask:

- Was it made for a special reason, such as propaganda?

- Under what conditions was the film made?

- Was the film shot 'live', as it happened, or was the film a later reconstruction, using actors?

- Does it contradict or support other forms of evidence?

- Was the director able to film everything he or she wished?

- What questions does the film help to answer?

EXERCISES

The following sources are taken from films and newsreels which are linked with setting up the Welfare State, during and after the second world war.

6 Which commentary (9i or 9j) do you think people in the 1940s would have found easier to understand, as an explanation of what was to be done after the war? Explain your answer.

7 What can a historian learn from a feature film, such as *Love on the Dole*?

8 (a) Source 9j was made by the Ministry of Information. Is this extract only giving information? Explain your answer.
(b) If not, why has this sequence been included in the film?
(c) What does this tell you about the problems of using cinema films as evidence?

SOURCE 9i

(Sir William Beveridge describes his scheme for a welfare state to film cameras in 1942)

The report proposes, first, an all-in scheme of **social insurance**, providing for all citizens and their families all cash benefits needed for security in return for a single weekly contribution by one insurance stamp.

The report proposes, second, a scheme of children's allowances to be paid both when the responsible parent is earning and when he is not.

The report proposes, third, an all-in scheme of medical treatment of all kinds for all citizens.

SOURCE 9j

(*The Dawn Guard*, a Ministry of Information film, 1941. Two actors played the parts of an old and a young soldier.)

Old soldier:
Look at us here, now, still doing the things we've done all our lives – ploughing, sowing, reaping, ploughing, milking, hay-making, a game of darts maybe, market on Thursdays, all the things we've been used to always. And here's someone

[Hitler] trying to take them away from us, trying to smash our lives . . .

This I do know, we ain't never properly appreciated all these things we got so used to, and the peace that went with them, free to come and free to go. It's the liberty we had and never thought about we gotta fight for, to get our lives back to where they was . . .

Young soldier:
Ah, that's all right, Bob, but that isn't enough. We've been doing some hard thinking lately and we haven't got to stop when this job's finished [i.e. when the war is over] . . .

We've made a fine big war effort. Well, when it's over, we've got to see to it that we make a fine big peace effort. There's no two ways about it. Won't go back now we've made a start. Look at that Dunkirk. There wasn't no unemployed there. Every man had a job to do and he done it. That's got to be what we see they have in peacetime. A job.

There'll be work enough too when this lot's over, building up something new and better than what's been destroyed. There mustn't be no more chaps hanging around for work what don't come. No more slums, neither. No more dirty, filthy back streets and no more half-starved kids with no room to play in. We gotta pack them all up and get moving out into the brightness of the sun. Fresh air and sunshine don't cost nothing. We can't go back into the old way of living.

A shot from Love on the Dole, *a 1941 feature film. It was a story about unemployed cotton-workers in Lancashire between the wars.*

—10—
Fiction

'Fiction' means something that has been invented or made up, so it covers a variety of different types of evidence. In this chapter, we shall look at novels, poems and ballads.

Novels: education

Often, the authors of nineteenth-century novels based their stories on what they saw about them. Consequently, they can provide detailed descriptions of people, buildings, events, people's clothes and relationships – and even of the way they spoke.

On the other hand, authors may have exaggerated things to make them interesting and exciting for their readers. They had to make sure that their books would sell, so they had to include features that would appeal.

Some authors were writing for a particular purpose. For instance, they might have wanted to show how badly off one group of people was. The workhouse sections of Charles Dickens' book *Oliver Twist*, were based on the author's knowledge of the workhouse in Chatham, Kent.

These points are illustrated in the next section, which examines schools and education in the nineteenth century.

SOURCE 10a

(*Hard Times* by Charles Dickens, 1854. It is based on the town of Preston. This extract begins with a description of the schoolmaster, Thomas Gradgrind)

Thomas Gradgrind, sir. A man of realities. A man of facts and calculations. A man who proceeds upon the principle that two and two are four, and nothing over, and who is not to be talked into allowing for anything over . . . With a rule and a pair of scales, and the multiplication table always in his pocket, sir, ready to weigh and measure any parcel of human nature, and tell you exactly what it comes to . . .

. . . Thomas Gradgrind now presented Thomas Gradgrind to the little **pitchers** before him, who were to be filled so full of facts . . .

He seemed a kind of cannon loaded to the muzzle with facts, and prepared to blow them clean out of the regions of childhood at one discharge . . .

'Girl number twenty,' said Mr Gradgrind, squarely pointing with his square forefinger, 'I don't know that girl. Who is that girl?'

'Sissy Jupe, sir,' explained number twenty, blushing, standing up, and curtseying.

'Sissy is not a name,' said Mr Gradgrind. 'Don't call yourself Sissy. Call yourself Cecilia.'

'It's father as calls me Sissy, sir,' returned the young girl in a trembling voice, and with another curtsey.

'Then he has no business to do it,' said Mr Gradgrind. 'Tell him he mustn't. Cecilia Jupe. Let me see. What is your father?'

'He belongs to the horse-riding, if you please, sir.'

Mr Gradgrind frowned, and waved off the objectionable calling with his hand.

'We don't want to know anything about that, here. You mustn't tell us about that, here. Your father breaks horses, don't he?'

'If you please, sir, when they can get any to break, they do break horses in the ring, sir.'

'You mustn't tell us about the ring, here. Very well, then. Describe your father as a horsebreaker. He doctors horses, I dare say?'

'Oh yes, sir.'

'Very well, then. He is a veterinary surgeon, a **farrier**, and horse-breaker. Give me your definition of a horse.'

(Sissy Jupe thrown into the greatest alarm by this demand.)

'Girl number twenty unable to define a horse!' said Mr Gradgrind, for the general behoof of all the little pitchers. 'Girl number twenty possessed of no facts, in reference to one of the commonest of animals! Some boy's definition of a horse. Bitzer, yours.' . . .

'**Quadruped**. **Graminivorous**. Forty teeth, namely twenty-four grinders, four eye-teeth, and twelve incisive. Sheds coat in the spring; in marshy countries, sheds hoofs, too. Hoofs hard, but requiring to be shod with iron. Age known by marks in mouth.' Thus (and much more) Bitzer.

'Now girl number twenty,' said Mr Gradgrind. 'You know what a horse is.'

(*The Handy Book of Object Lessons*, 1873. This was a book of lessons for teachers to teach. On the left are the facts to be taught. On the right are ideas of how to do it)

20   NOTES OF LESSONS ON FAMILIAR OBJECTS.

THE HORSE.

MATTER.	METHOD.
I. Where found.	What animal do we employ to draw carts, carriages, &c. **The Horse.**
Horses are found nearly all over the world. They are met with in a wild state in South America, having been introduced into that country by the Spaniards. Probably horses came originally from Egypt.	
II. Description of the various kinds.	
(*a*) WELSH PONY. Found chiefly in Wales, hence its name. It is a small kind, and has long shaggy hair.	
(*b*) SHETLAND PONY. Found, as its name implies, in the Shetland Islands.[1] It is very similar in appearance to the Welsh variety.	[1] Shew them on the map.
(*c*) The CART HORSE. Probably a breed obtained from the Dutch and Belgian horses, those of Flanders being highly esteemed at the present day.[2]	[2] In order to shew the strength of these horses, refer to the brewers' drays of London and other large towns. Some horses of this breed will draw as much as three tons.
(*d*) The RACER. The most slender species; has long, thin legs, a short mane, sleek skin, and erect ears. One horse of this kind, called, on account of its great fleetness "Flying Childers," is said to have run a mile in a minute.[4]	
(*e*) The HUNTER. Combines, to a certain extent, the agility of the race horse with the strength of the cart horse[5].	[4] An idea of this great speed may be obtained by referring to an express train which generally travels 45 or 50 miles per hour.
(*f*) The CARRIAGE HORSE. Similar to the hunter.	[5] Shew why these qualities are necessary in a hunter—agility, to leap fences, &c.— strength, to endure the fatigue of a long run.
(*g*) The PACK HORSE. Very rare at the present time. They were formerly used as beasts of burden in this country, their load being slung across their back.[6]	[6] Refer to the condition of our roads at the time (about 200 years ago), when these horses were so much used.
(*h*) The ARAB. These are greatly prized by their masters, so much so that an Arab would rather part with anything than sell his horse. They are particularly affectionate, especially to the children of the family. Probably this is the result of great kindness shewn them by their master.[7] The Arabs preserve the genealogies of their horses as carefully as we do those of our families.	[7] Draw from this a lesson of humanity, and contrast such kindness with the brutal treatment some of our English horses receive.
III. Habits.	
Horses are very sagacious and become much attached to their masters. They breathe *only* through their nostrils, the mouth never being found open, even after severe exercise, unless opened by the action of the bit. It is this fact which accounts for the expanding[8] of their nostrils after violent exertion.	
IV. Uses.	[8] What does expanding mean? (Illus. by a blown bladder.)
Horses are used by most nations as beasts of burden and draught. They are also ridden. In Egypt they were formerly used to draw chariots.	

EXERCISES

1 (a) Do you think Mr Gradgrind would have taught lessons like the one in Source 10b? Explain how you decided.
(b) Why does Dickens call the children 'pitchers'?

(c) What can you learn about teachers' attitudes from Source 10a that you cannot learn from Source 10b?

(d) Do you think Dickens knew how nineteenth-century teachers taught? Explain how you decided.

2 From Source 10a, what do you think Dickens thought of teachers? Explain your answer.

FEBRUARY.— Cutting Weather — Squally.

This cartoon of 1839 by Cruikshank, shows what people thought about teachers.

Poetry: climbing boys

Many hundreds of poems also give historians a detailed insight into the life of the times. The poems below are both about the children who were used as chimney sweeps.

They were known as climbing boys because they had to climb up the inside of chimneys to sweep them clean. In the nineteenth century, a campaign to put a stop to this sort of work was led by Lord Shaftesbury.

SOURCE 10c

(Elizabeth Turner: *The Daisy*, 1806)

The Chimney Sweeper

'Sweep! sweep! sweep! sweep!' cries little Jack,
With brush and bag upon his back.
And black from head to foot;
While daily, as he goes along,
'Sweep! sweep! sweep! sweep!' is all his song
    Beneath his load of soot.
But then he was not always black.,
Oh, no! he once was pretty Jack,
    And had a kind papa;
But, silly child! he ran to play
Too far from home, a long, long way,
    And did not ask Mamma.

So he was lost, and now must creep
Up chimneys, crying 'Sweep! sweep! sweep!'

SOURCE 10d

(William Blake: *Songs of Innocence*, 1789)

The Chimney Sweeper

When my mother died I was very young,
And my father sold me while yet my tongue
Could scarcely cry ''weep! 'weep! 'weep! 'weep!'
So your chimneys I sweep, and in soot I sleep.

There's little Tom Dacre, who cried when his head,
That curl'd like a lamb's back, was shav'd: so I said
'Hush, Tom! never mind it, for when your head's bare
'You know that the soot cannot spoil your white hair.'

And so he was quiet, & that very night,
As Tom was a-sleeping, he had such a sight!
That thousands of sweepers, Dick, Joe, Ned & Jack,
Were all of them lock'd up in coffins of black.

And by came an Angel who had a bright key,
And he open'd the coffins and set them all free;
Then down a green plain leaping, laughing, they run,
And wash in a river, and shine in the Sun.

Then naked & white, all their bags left behind,
They rise upon clouds and sport in the wind;
And the Angel told Tom, if he'd be a good boy,
He'd have God for a father, & never want joy.

And so Tom awoke; and we rose in the dark,

And got with our bags & our brushes to work.
Tho' the morning was cold, Tom was happy &
warm;
So if all do their duty they need not fear harm.

EXERCISES

3 (a) According to Source 10c, how did
Jack become a sweep?
(b) According to Source 10d, how did
the boy become a sweep?
4 What does Source 10d tell you about
religion?
5 (a) What are these poems intended to
make their readers feel about chimney
sweeps? Explain your answer.
(b) How do the authors create these
feelings? Quote from the passage in your
answer.

In contrast to the poems, now read an
extract from a famous novel called *The
Water Babies*. It tells the story of a chimney-
sweep employed by a bully called Mr
Grimes.

SOURCE 10e

(Charles Kingsley: *The Water Babies*, 1863)

Once upon a time there was a little chimney-
sweep, and his name was Tom . . . He could not
read nor write, and did not care to do either;
and he never washed himself, for there was no
water up the court where he lived.

He had never been taught to say his prayers.
He had never heard of God, or Christ, except in
words which you never have heard, and which it
would have been well if he had never heard.

He cried half his time, and laughed the other
half. He cried when he had to climb the dark
flues, rubbing his poor knees and elbows raw;
and when the soot got into his eyes, which it did
every day in the week; and when his master beat
him, which he did every day in the week; and
when he had not enough to eat, which happened
every day in the week likewise. And he laughed
the other half of the day, when he was tossing
halfpennies with the other boys, or playing
leapfrog over the posts, or bowling stones at the

horses' legs as they trotted by, which last was
excellent fun, when there was a wall at hand
behind which to hide.

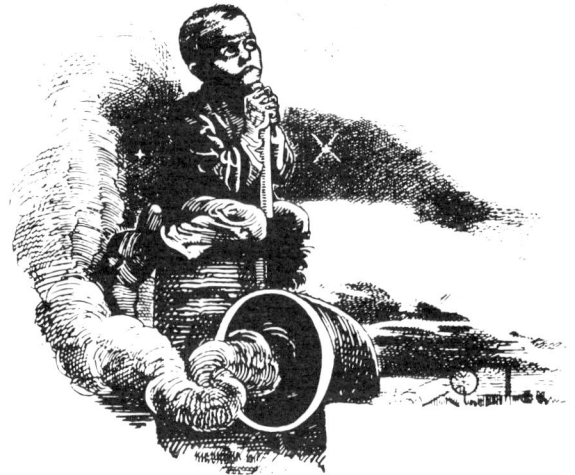

A drawing from an 1898 edition of The Water Babies.

EXERCISES

6 (a) Compare the view of chimney
sweeps in Source 10e with the view
given in Sources 10c and 10d. What is
the same, and what is different?
(b) Which of these sources do you think
presents the most accurate picture?
Explain how you decided.
(c) What other sources might you use to
see whether your chosen source actually
is accurate?

Ballads

There are two main forms of nineteenth-
century ballad. The first is the broadside
ballad. These were composed for singing
in a street or tavern, a concert hall or at a
dinner. Later in the century, they were
sung in music halls.

Broadsides were best known in London.
Some were based on traditional songs or
used traditional tunes. Others were simply
made up because they would attract an
audience in the street.

LONG-SONG SELLER

(Jon Raven: *Songs of a Changing World*, published in 1972)

Wife for sale

This is to give notice that Bandy Leg Lett
Will sell his wife Sally for what he can get,
At twelve o'clock certain the sale'll begin
So all you gay[1] fellows be there with your tin.

Chorus:
And it's ding a-dong, ding a-dong, oh ah, oh ah,
ding a-dong, ding a-dong.
Well it's ding a-dong, ding a-dong, oh ah, oh ah,
ding a-dong, ding a-dong.

For Sally's good looking and sound as a bell,
If you'd only once heard her you'd know that
right well,
Her bakes bread quite handy and eats it all up,
Brews beer like a good'un and drinks every sup.

Her wears men's breeches[2] so all the folks say,
But Lett should not let her have all her own way.
Her swears like a trooper and fights like a cock,
And has gin[3] her old feller just many a hard
knock.

So all you young fellows as wanting a wife,
Come and bid for old Sally the plague of Lett's
life.
At twelve in the morning the sale'll begin;
So you as wants splicin'[4] be there with your tin.

[1] gay = *jolly*   [2] breeches = *trousers*
[3] gin = *given*   [4] splicin' = *married*

These broadsides were often written to make money by selling copies of them. Long-song sellers sold large sheets with three songs on them for 1d. They covered practically every subject, including topical ones. Some were very rude.

These broadsides can provide historians with a flavour of life at the time, especially among poorer people. After all, less educated people did not write novels, or newspapers. So ballads give us some idea of what amused them and how they felt about things.

In this way, ballads provide an insight into attitudes which people had at the time. The first example tells us something of men's attitudes towards women.

The second type of ballad is more like a folk song. These were not usually written down, but were made up and sung in pubs or at work. They often followed tunes or styles which were typical of a particular part of the country.

Such ballads provide a rare direct view of ordinary working people's attitudes to their lives and work in the eighteenth and nineteenth centuries. The next ballad sings the praises of one of the famous inventors of the late eighteenth century.

SOURCE 10g

(Jon Raven: *Victoria's Inferno*, 1978)

John Wilkinson

You workmen of Bilston and Bradley draw near,
Sit down and take your pipes and my song you
shall hear.
I sing not of war or the state of the nation,
Such subjects as these produce nought but
vexation[1].

But before I proceed any more with my tale,
You shall all drink my health in a bumper of ale.
Fill it up, and without any further parade,
John Wilkinson, boys, that supporter of trade.

May all his endeavours be crowned with success,
And his works, ever growing, prosperity bless.
May his comforts increase with the length of his
days
And his fame shine as bright as his famous blaze.

That the wood of old England would fail, did
appear
And though iron was scarce because charcoal
was dear,
By puddling[2] and stamping[3] he cured that evil,
So the Swedes and the Russians may go to the
divil.

Our thundering cannon so frequently burst,
A mischief so great he prevented the first.
And now it is well known they never miscarry,
But drive all our foes with a blast to old Harry.

Then let each jolly fellow take hold of his glass,
And drink to the health of his friend and his lass.
May we always have plenty of good beer and
pence,
And Wilkinson's fame blaze a thousand years
hence.

[1] vexation = *worry*   [2] puddling = *stirring molten
iron*   [3] stamping = *forming bars of iron*

John Wilkinson.

EXERCISES

7 (a) What does Source 10f tell you about men's attitudes towards women?
(b) Wives *were* sometimes sold in this way. What sources would an historian need to prove this?
8 (a) What attitude is shown towards John Wilkinson in the second ballad?
(b) Why might working people praise him so greatly?
(c) Where do you think this song was planned to be sung? Explain how you decided.
9 (a) Why do you think such ballads were popular in the nineteenth century?
(b) How would a historian in the next century learn about the lives of poorer people in the twentieth century? Explain how you decided.

—11—
Statistics

Statistics can provide us with some of the 'hard' evidence that other sources lack. Letters or photographs may help us to understand how people felt or thought; statistics can tell us what was actually happening. For example, they can demonstrate a trend, such as an increase in population. This is shown on the graph below.

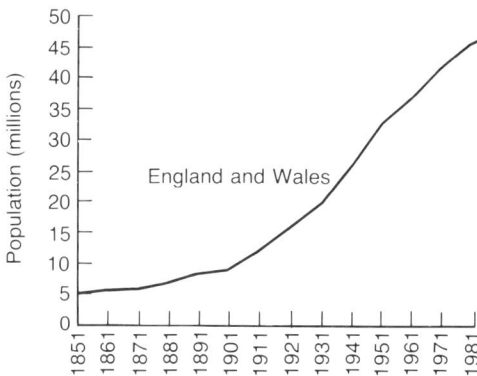

England and Wales

However, the bare statistics do not begin to tell us *why* things happened as they did. It is possible that other statistics may do this.

For example, the next graph shows the birth and death rates from 1700 to 1980. Clearly, a rise in the birth rate or a fall in the death rate may help to explain an increase in population.

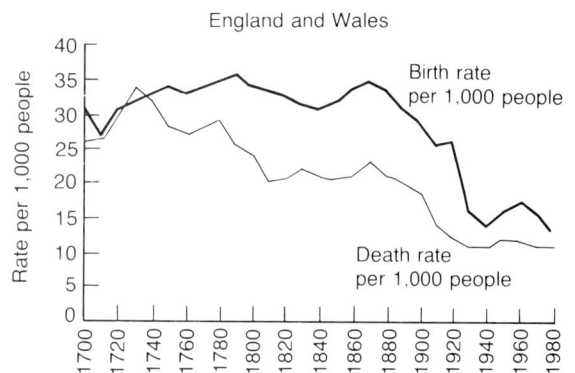

At that point, statistics become of less value. They cannot help us to learn *why* the birth rate went up nor *why* the death rate went down. For this information, the historian would need other evidence. Therefore, as a source, statistics are really only of value in summarising information.

Even then, eighteenth and nineteenth century statistics have to be treated with care. The first **census** was not taken until 1801, so most population figures before that date are estimates.

Even after 1801, the census returns cannot be taken as wholly accurate. It was not compulsory to register the births of children until 1836.

So earlier figures are based on parish records. These were the vicar's records of whom he had baptised, married or buried in his parish. Often, they were not complete and they did not include those who had moved away. For several reasons, therefore, statistics must be regarded as a very limited form of historical evidence, as the next two sections illustrate.

Newgate Prison

EXERCISES

Study the four written sources below, together with the three pictures in this section. Then answer these questions:

1 (a) What can you learn from Source 11a?
   (b) What other statistics would you need to understand Source 11a fully?
2 Which of all these sources gives you
   (a) the most and (b) the least factual information about Newgate Prison? Explain your answer.
3 Which of them gives you (a) the most and (b) the least understanding of what it must have been like in Newgate Prison in the late eighteenth and nineteenth centuries? Explain your answer.

SOURCE 11a

(Prisoners passing through Newgate, 1785–6)

Hanged   61
Transported   294
Whipped   176
Burnt   1
Died in Newgate   16
Acquitted   613
Total: 1 325

Total English executions in 1785 (estimated): 3300

SOURCE 11b

(George Agar Ellis MP: *Diary*, 1816)

We ... went all over Newgate, which is dreadfully crowded, and the prisoners not properly classed. The infirmary was quite horrid; a moderate sized room and very hot; with twelve sick persons in it, and two dead ones. Saw

the boys' school. There is one boy named Leary of thirteen who has been in Newgate twenty times, and been four times under sentence of death. Also four boys, one of nine, one of eleven, one of thirteen, and one of fourteen who have been altogether in Newgate between 70 and 80 times. These all keep their women. Such a scene of youthful **depravity** is almost inconceivable . . .

SOURCE 11c

(William Cobbett: *Parliamentary Debates*. This is from a committee report of 1814)

No bedding is provided: the poorer description of prisoners sleep on the boards, between two rugs given by the city; those who can afford it hire beds at sixpence the night, from persons who carry on this traffic with the prison. The allowance of food to debtors is fourteen ounces of bread a day, and eight stone of meat in every week, divided amongst all; this quantity never varies with the numbers . . .

SOURCE 11d

(Elizabeth Fry, quoted in J Gibson: *John Howard and Elizabeth Fry*, 1971)

The begging, swearing, **gaming**, fighting, singing, dancing, dressing-up in men's clothes were too bad to be described, so that we did not think it suitable to take a young person within.

A prisoner being flogged in Newgate Prison, early nineteenth century.

Elizabeth Fry with female prisoners in Newgate, 1823.

The exercise yard at Newgate, 1872.

The establishment of the Metropolitan Police

EXERCISES

4 (a) Study Source 11e. List those crimes which increased by 1.5% or more.

(b) List those crimes which decreased by 1.5% or more.

(c) What is the total decrease in crimes committed?

(d) What is the total increase in population?

(e) What conclusions might you draw from these statistics?

5 Now, read Sources 11f and 11g, both taken from secondary sources. How do they help to explain the statistics in Source 11e?

SOURCE 11e

(Detected crimes committed in the Metropolitan Police area)

	1825	1835
Felonies	45.14	48.83
Common Assault	18.13	13.82
Larceny[1]	8.08	10.19
Unlawful Possession	2.04	4.00
Issuing or Possessing Base Coins[2]	2.69	3.69
Soldiers, tried by Court Martial	2.51	2.62
Fraud	3.41	2.39
Assaults on Police Constables	–	1.94
Assaults on Women and Children	2.00	1.16
Misdemeanour in Workhouse	0.50	0.93
Begging or Sleeping in the Open Air	0.50	0.77
Unlawful Collection of Dust	–	0.61
Wilful Damage	0.51	0.61
Drunk and Disorderly	0.56	0.55
Conspiracy to Defraud[3]	0.41	0.55
Cutting or Maiming	0.36	0.47
Illegally Pawning[4]	0.24	0.38
Excise Offences[5]	0.46	0.30
Indecent Exposure of the Person	0.46	0.30
Dog Stealing	0.12	0.24
Furious Driving and Insolence to Passengers	0.15	0.15
Leaving Families Chargeable to Parish	0.15	0.15
Abduction[6]	0.08	0.08
Unnatural Assaults	0.08	0.08
Bastardy	0.08	0.08
Cruelty to Animals	1.46	0.08
Keeping Brothels	0.02	0.08
Stealing Fruit, Plants or Trees, etc.	1.00	0.07
Trespassing, Fishing, Poaching Game, etc.	1.00	0.06
Obtaining Money by False Pretences	0.05	0.05
Total Number of Crimes Committed	317 214	201 416
Total Population of London	1 416 407	1 803 214

[1] larceny = robbery of goods or money
[2] base coins = forged coins (of inferior metal)
[3] conspiracy to defraud = planning to cheat someone of money
[4] illegally pawning = selling someone else's goods to a pawnbroker
[5] excise offences = smuggling (or avoiding customs duties)
[6] abduction = kidnapping

SOURCE 11f

(*The Story of our Police*, HMSO)

[London,] a city of 1½ million [had] about one policeman to every 3 000 people (today London has one policeman to about every 300 people). In addition to the police, there were also 4 500 watchmen, all more or less 'proper Charlies'.

Sir Robert Peel became Home Secretary in 1822. He believed that it was better to prevent crime from happening rather than to catch and punish people after they had committed a crime ... He said that he wanted to show people that 'liberty does not consist in having your houses robbed by organised gangs of thieves'. It was seven years before he introduced a 'Bill for improving the Police in and near the Metropolis'.

In 1829 the Metropolitan Police Act was passed ... Over 3 000 men were recruited for the new police force. They had to be under 35 years of age, in good health and strong, at least 5 ft 7 ins tall, able to read and write, and with a written recommendation as to good character. Peel and the two Police Commissioners wanted the force to be a really good body of men.

A large number of policemen on the streets meant that criminals had to think twice before they committed a crime. They ran a bigger risk of being caught. The type of person employed as a policeman was also much better, and this led to more crimes being solved.

A SLAP AT THE CHARLEYS or a Tarm & Jerry lark

This cartoon showed Sir Robert Peel getting rid of the night watchmen, known as Charlies.

SOURCE 11g

(C P Hill: *British Economic and Social History*, 1970)

In 1829 there arrived the Metropolitan Police Force organised by Sir Robert Peel to keep order in London. The new force, with headquarters at Scotland Yard, was essentially a civilian one, armed only with wooden truncheons and wearing, at first, top hats and blue frock-coats. Most Londoners greeted these 'Peelers' or 'Bobbies' with derision seeing them as a new instrument to destroy the liberties of the subject. But they were quickly accepted.

From the very start it was clear their [main] purpose was to prevent crime. The criminals of London paid a high tribute to their efficiency by migrating in some numbers to the larger provincial towns which in turn established their own forces ... ; whereupon the criminals moved to the smaller towns and countryside.

These exercises should also have made you think about who compiles statistics – and why they do it. Often, they are put together by governments to provide information. Sometimes, this is for planning purposes; for example, population figures are essential for working out how many new schools will be needed.

Statistics can also be used to see whether government policies are working. Each Christmas, the police are keen to establish how many drunken drivers have been caught. In the case of the crime figures (Source 11e), the government wanted to know if its new policy was working.

Finally, statistics can be helpful in planning changes of policy. If the crime rate gets worse, the government may wish to introduce new laws or changes to the police system. So, in considering the value of statistics, the historian must take account of their *purpose*.

—12—
Oral History

'Oral' literally means 'spoken'. So oral history is the name given to the history that is spoken by people talking about their experiences of historical events. It is an increasingly popular form of history.

It gives many people the chance to be a historian, by recording what they are told, and thus adding to the total sum of historical knowledge. It also gives others a chance to tell us what they know and feel about events in their lifetime.

This can be a very helpful form of history for learning how ordinary people were affected by national or world events. In contrast, textbooks usually only give an overall view of what happened. Secondly, people can provide details of local events that might otherwise eventually be lost. In addition, an individual talking can give an immediacy and a vividness to events.

On the other hand, we all know that our memories are far from perfect. We are liable to forget things and to confuse details. This is especially the case if people are being asked to talk about things that happened a long time ago.

Sometimes, several people talking about the same period or event will have different views of it. So it may be that a combination of several different people's views will be needed.

Setting up an oral history assignment

An oral history assignment can be an interesting way of completing a GCSE coursework assignment. Some of the stages that you will need to go through are outlined here.

Choosing a topic

Do not choose a subject that is too wide, such as 'Transport in the twentieth century'. On the other hand, it must not be too limited, such as 'Memories of Beesands Rovers F.C. in 1947'.

Finding people to interview

Try to make sure that your subjects are willing to take part, and are likely to remember details. Most important, make sure you have talked to them in outline about what you are doing, and that they know what questions you will be asking them. If possible, get a copy of your questions to them in advance. It is best to approach someone you know and trust, not a stranger.

IT'LL **ONLY** TAKE A COUPLE OF MINUTES....

Drawing up your questions

This is the hardest, and the most important, part of your work. First, write a list of the general subject areas you hope to learn about. Sort this into a sensible order.

Then, draw up your questions on each area. Make sure these are brief, clear and to the point. Avoid asking too many questions. Make each of them open-ended, giving your subjects a chance to talk.

If you ask questions that can be answered by one word, or by 'yes' or 'no', you won't learn much. Remember too not to make the questions too personal: this is an exercise in writing history, not collecting gossip.

I CAN'T PRINT **THAT**, MUM....

Have a trial run

Start with a member of your family; it will probably be best to choose someone aged under fifty. Try to make a recording of the interview, and don't worry if things don't go too well. Your first effort will provide vital practice.

Conducting your interviews

Make sure you record the answers carefully. Use a cassette recorder if you can, as it will be hard to write down all of a reply, and notes can easily be confused. Make sure your subjects speak clearly, and ask them to repeat or explain more fully anything you don't understand.

MUMBLE MUMBLE RUMBLE ...BURP

Writing up your research

If you simply produce a written version of your recorded interviews, this is called a transcript. This will be useful, and may well form an appendix to your assignment.

The bulk of your work will be a write-up of your interview(s), in which:

- you summarise what you have learnt (using quotes, where relevant)

- you comment on what you have heard, comparing views of the event or period that you have got from different people

- you compare the results of your findings with what you have researched from other sources, such as books or articles.

Finishing off

Make sure you include all the important 'beginning and end' parts to your assignment:

- a title page

- a list of contents

- an introduction, in which you explain why you chose the topic and what you are trying to find out

- a bibliography, in which you list your sources of information, including people

- a conclusion, in which you explain whether you found out what you hoped to, and how your research could have been improved.

The next extract is an example of an oral history interview. The subject was born in 1909, and is talking about family life in the 1920s. This extract comes at the start of the interview. It lasts three minutes of an interview which took about an hour.

Interviewer:
Can you tell me – did you have any particular rules at home?
Mrs P:
What sort of rules?
Interviewer:
Well, about perhaps mealtimes or how you should behave.
Mrs P:
Oh yes, we had, well, you see, er 1920, did you say?
Interviewer:
Well, just about when you were little.
Mrs P:
Yes, I was just trying to work out how many we were then. About five of us. Yes, we had strict rules. My father was a carpenter and he was one of those, er, er very hard-working and very given to his job. He used to go to work at six o'clock and he didn't come home to breakfast but he came home to lunch, you see. And we came home from school, those that were at school, also came home to lunch, you see, because no school meals or anything like that. And er, yes I don't think we were kept to a rigid rule about going to bed, except that when he came in he didn't want us around. You see, we lived in a small terrace house . . .
Interviewer:
Where was this?
Mrs P:
In Hertfordshire.
Interviewer:
In a village?
Mrs P:
Yes, actually it wasn't much of a village. It was, erm, sort of more-or-less controlled by a big firm of paper-makers, Dickinsons and, well, I should think two out of three worked at Dickinsons but, erm, my father didn't of course. It was paper, you know, printing envelopes and things like that. But only one

of us went to work there cos my father and mother didn't like it much, you know, I don't know why. Well, I suppose they looked round at the others and saw what they were like and didn't want us to be the same. But erm we all started, erm we all had a job down there and then we moved out, you know. Dad and Mum moved us out for some reason or other, erm, well, I know it was mine because I did take up the language rather strongly, which was very prominent in the factory, you know. It er it, it was, it was a way of speaking in the factory, you see and I used to come home and my father was very, very strict. He was a Baptist, he never swore and he never drank. I don't want you to think he was a prude. He wasn't. He really was a lively man, you know, but, well that had to stop, so he shifted me out of that. Not before, erm my sister did this as well, she was three years younger than me, not before she and I had been put in, they used to have erm, the firms used to have evening classes and we started up shorthand and typewriting in the factory evening class and then as soon as Dad and Mum knew that we were going to take to it, they moved us over to a private school which was a shilling.

Home life of a poor family, 1923

EXERCISES

1 What was the interviewer trying to find out?
2 (a) What problems did the interviewer face?
   (b) What can you learn about interviewing from this?
3 If you were the interviewer, what would you do at this point?
4 Make a list of five key questions you could have asked this woman about rules.

—13—

Case Study: Factory Conditions in the Nineteenth Century

This chapter takes the form of a single exercise. You are asked to compare a variety of different sources and apply the ideas you have studied in this book.

SOURCE 13a

(*Poverty Knock*, sung by Tom Daniel, a Yorkshire weaver who died in 1970)

Up every morning at five.
I wonder that we keep alive.
Tired and yawnin' on the cold mornin',
It's back to the dreary old drive.

Chorus:

> Poverty, poverty knock!
> Me **loom** is a-sayin' all day.
> Poverty, poverty knock!
> Gaffer's[1] too skinny to pay.
> Poverty, poverty knock!
> Keepin' one eye on the clock.
> I know I can guttle[2]
> When I hear me shuttle
> Go: poverty, poverty knock!

Oh dear, we're goin' to be late.
Gaffer is stood at the gate.
We're out o'pocket, our wages they're docket;
We'll 'a' to buy grub on the slate.

An' when our wages they'll bring,
We're often short of a string.
While we are fratchin'[3] wi' gaffer for snatchin',
We know to his brass he will cling.

We've got to wet our own yarn
By dippin' it into the tarn[4],
It's wet an' soggy an' makes us feel groggy,
An' there's mice in that dirty old barn.

Oh dear, me poor 'ead it sings,
I should have woven three strings,
But threads are breakin' and my back is achin'.
Oh dear, I wish I had wings.

Sometimes a shuttle flies out,
Gives some poor woman a clout.
There she lies bleedin', but nobody's heedin'.
Who's goin' t'carry her out?

Tuner should tackle me loom
'E'd rather sit himself down,
'E's far too busy a-courtin' our Lizzie,
An' ah cannot get 'im to come.

[1] gaffer = *the owner*   [2] guttle = *eat greedily*
[3] fratchin' = *quarrelling*   [4] tarn = *lake*

SOURCE 13b

(*The Scotsman*, August 5 1826)

A boy or girl of from 12 to 14 years of age can with ease attend to two power-looms, and can produce three times as much excellently woven cloth as could be produced by the best hand weaver. In 1818, there were about 2 000 power-looms in Manchester, Stockport and the immediate [area]; in 1821, 5 733; and in July, 1825, in the parish of Manchester alone upward of 20 000.

SOURCE 13c

Children working in a cotton mill.

SOURCE 13d

(Evidence of Operatives, Clergymen and Others before Mr Sadler's Committee, 1832)

BENTLEY, ELIZABETH; age twenty-three; examined 4th June 1832; began to work, as a **doffer**, when six years old, in a flax mill, at Leeds.

What were your hours of labour? – From five in the morning, till nine at night, when they were thronged [busy].
For how long a time together have you worked that excessive length of time? – For about half a year.
What were your usual hours of labour, when you were not so thronged? – From six in the morning, till seven at night.
What time was allowed for your meals? – Forty minutes at noon.
Had you any time to get your breakfast, or drinking? – No, we got it as we could.
And when your work was bad, you had hardly any time to eat it at all? – No; we were obliged to leave it or to take it home, and when we did not take it, the overlooker took it, and gave it to his pigs.
Suppose you flagged a little, or were too late, what would they do? – Strap us.
Girls as well as boys? – Yes.
Have you ever been strapped? – Yes, severely.

SOURCE 13e

Mule-spinning in a cotton mill.

SOURCE 13f

(The Duke of Rutland: Journal of a Tour in the Northern Parts of Great Britain, published 1813. He is describing Dale's cotton mill at New Lanark in 1796)

Some idea may be formed of the benefits which he has conferred upon the community, when it is mentioned, that 1 800 persons derive employment under his **auspices**. He cloathes, he feeds them, and large as the number of his dependants is, there is not an individual who does not partake of the attention of his benevolent ... master.

Persons of all ages have the benefit of employment under him; old women, and even children afflicted with blindness, can obtain a **subsistence** by work. But above all, we were struck by the excellence of his arrangements with regard to the health, order, and morals of his work-people, in which his benevolence, not less than his good sense, was obvious.

His plan must indeed be considered as a model, and it furnishes a convincing proof that most of the objections to manufactures on the score of their injurious influence on the persons employed in them, may be obviated by management and attention. There are several schools in the manufactory, adapted to the different ages of the children.

(Lord Shaftesbury: *Journal*, December 25 1843)

Rose before six to prayer and meditation. Ah, blessed God, how many in the mills and factories have risen at four, on this day even, to toil and suffering!

SOURCE 13h

In a cotton mill, 1851.

SOURCE 13i

(*Second Report . . . on the Employment of Children in Factories*, 1833. This extract deals with injuries at work)

James Adam, aged fifty-eight. At mills for seventeen or eighteen years; previously a weaver; lost about half of fore-arm six weeks ago, at Gordon's new mill; still on full pay.

David Salmond, aged twelve. Went to Inch mill in seventh or eighth year, and four weeks after lost four fingers of left hand; allowed half pay for four weeks after.

Jean M'Cabe, aged twenty-six. Attended mills for ten years; loss of right thumb, with injury of the muscles of the palm, producing contraction of the fingers; was unable to work for some time after; had no pay or half pay, but received a gratuity of £1.

SOURCE 13j

Apprentice's indenture, 1801

English Factory Slaves. Pl.3 Their daily employment.—

Cartoon by Robert Cruikshank

A nineteenth century cartoonist, Cruikshank, gives his view of factory work.

EXERCISES

1 Write a list of the different types of sources that are represented by Sources 13a to 13k (diary, official record etc).
2 Are any of these sources secondary sources? Explain your answer.
3 Which of these sources provide you with:
(a) fact(s) only
(b) opinion(s) only
(c) a mixture of fact and opinions?
Where necessary, explain your decisions.
4 What conclusions can you draw *from these sources only* about:
(a) the hours of work in factories and mills;
(b) the employment of children;
(c) accidents and injuries in factories and mills?
5 (a) In what ways does Source 13f contradict the evidence of other sources?
(b) Why do you think the Duke of Rutland, in Source 13f, had a different view?
6 (a) Which of these sources provided you with the most information?
(b) Why do you think this was?
7 If you had to decide which is the *most* reliable evidence for nineteenth-century factory conditions, and which is the *least* reliable, which two sources would you choose and why?

Glossary

abortion ending a pregnancy
apprentice young person learning a trade or craft
arable land used for growing crops
auspices control

captions words under a cartoon
censored changed by having parts cut out
census official count of all the people in the country
Chartism political group campaigning for workers' rights
commentary words which accompany a film
commission group of people set up by the government to investigate a particular matter
consistent agreeing; not contradicting
contemporary from the same time
contradict disagree with

dame school private school run by an old woman
day labourer farm labourer who only got paid for each day he worked
decade ten years
depravity living in filthy and vicious surroundings
dissipated wasted
documentary film showing real events
doffer worker in a cotton mill

editorial newspaper article giving the newspaper's opinion
ethical moral
execration condemnation; criticism

farrier blacksmith

gaming gambling
ghost-writer person who writes an autobiography for someone
gosling young goose
graminivorous grass-eating

intimidation the use of fear to make someone do something

larceny stealing property
loom machine for weaving yarn

malevolent hoping for something bad to happen to someone else
memoirs person's account of his or her own life
minutes record of what happened at a meeting

narrative story

orators speakers

pasture land used for animals to graze
pauper poor person
pitchers empty vessels, such as jugs or jars
prejudice opinion without good reason
propaganda method of spreading opinions, and getting people to believe them

quadruped a four legged animal

radical person who campaigned for major political or economic changes

sabre heavy, curved sword
social insurance national scheme to ensure that the sick and unemployed received money
subsistence living on a bare minimum

tenant farmer person who pays to farm someone else's land
tract small pamphlet
traitor person who betrays his or her country
TUC Trades Union Congress

venereal disease sexually transmitted disease

Index